Child Observation
for the Early Years

Child Observation

for the Early Years

Second edition

Ioanna Palaiologou

SAGE | LearningMatters

Los Angeles | London | New Delhi
Singapore | Washington DC

Los Angeles | London | New Delhi
Singapore | Washington DC

www.learningmatters.co.uk

Learning Matters
An imprint of SAGE Publications Ltd
1 Oliver's Yard
55 City Road
London EC1Y 1SP

SAGE Publications Inc.
2455 Teller Road
Thousand Oaks, California 91320

SAGE Publications India Pvt Ltd
B 1/I 1 Mohan Cooperative Industrial Area
Mathura Road
New Delhi 110 044

SAGE Publications Asia-Pacific Pte Ltd
3 Church Street
#10-04 Samsung Hub
Singapore 049483

Editor: Amy Thornton
Development editor: Geoff Barker
Production controller: Chris Marke
Project management: Deer Park Productions,
Tavistock, Devon
Marketing manager: Catherine Slinn
Cover design: Code 5 Design
Typeset by: TW Typesetting, Plymouth, Devon
Printed by: MPG Books Group, Bodmin, Cornwall

First published in 2008 by Learning Matters Ltd.
Reprinted twice in 2009
Second edition published in 2012

This book was previously available as 'Childhood Observation'
written by Ioanna Palaiologou, with Gill Goodliff and Lyn Trodd
as series editors. This new edition has been revised and the
author has added three new chapters.

Library of Congress Control Number: 2012934563

British Library Cataloguing in Publication data

A catalogue record for this book is available from the
British Library

ISBN 978-0-85725-860-1
ISBN 978-0-85725-745-1 (pbk)

Contents

The author   vi

Dedication   vi

Acknowledgements   vii

Introduction: Policy context and observation   1

1   The pedagogy of early years   10

2   The role of observation in early years   38

3   Observation techniques   57

4   Analysing and documenting observations   84

5   Ethical implications   98

6   Observing for development   107

7   Observing for research   119

8   Observing for the curriculum   132

Summary: Early years workforce and observation   149

References   158

Appendix   172

Index   173

The author

Dr Ioanna Palaiologou (CPsychol) is a lecturer and researcher in the Centre for Educational Studies at the University of Hull. She was originally qualified as an early years teacher and child psychologist. She then studied for her Masters degree in Educational Psychology and completed her PhD at Nottingham University investigating young children's responses to a cognitive-oriented intervention programme using observations. Ioanna worked as a researcher and lecturer on Early Childhood Studies degree courses at the University of Wales Swansea and Nottingham Trent University. In 2004 she joined the University of Hull and is currently leading the Masters in Early Childhood Studies at the University of Hull. Ioanna is also a Chartered Psychologist of the British Psychological Society with specialism on child development and learning theories. Her main research interests are the field of psychological theories of learning and their impact on the development of pedagogy in early years education, and child development with particular interest in language development and literacy in the early years.

Dedication

To my boys: Demos, Haralampos, George and Harry for the happiness they have offered me and continue to offer me all these years.

Acknowledgements

The first edition of this popular and well-received text was edited and published as part of the *Achieving Early Years Professional Status* series edited by Gill Goodliff and Lyn Trodd.

Gill Goodliff is a Senior Lecturer in Education and Head of Qualifications for Early Years at the Open University including the Sector-Endorsed Foundation Degree and BA Early Years. Gill is on the Committee of the National Network of Sector-Endorsed Foundation Degrees in Early Years, and from 2006 to 2012 has been involved in the development and delivery of four pathways leading to Early Years Professional Status. Gill has edited and contributed to a number of published core texts for early years practitioners. Her research interests centre on the professional identities of early years practitioners and young children's spirituality.

Lyn Trodd is Head of Partnerships and Ventures at the University of Hertfordshire. Lyn is the Chair of the National Network of Sector-Endorsed Foundation Degrees in Early Years. She was involved in the design of Early Years Professional Status, helped to pilot the Validation Pathway when it first became available and is currently part of two consortia offering EYPS provision in North London and the East of England. Lyn has published and edited a range of articles, national and international conference papers and books focusing on self-efficacy in the child and the practitioner, the professional identity and role of adults who work with young children and interprofessional working.

Every effort has been made to trace the copyright holders and to obtain their permission for the use of copyright material. The publisher and author will gladly receive any information enabling them to rectify any error or omission in subsequent editions.

Introduction: Policy context and observation

Through reading this introduction, you will:

- consider the changes in the early years sector;
- develop an understanding of the Early Years Foundation Stage;
- consider the provision for children aged 0–5;
- explore the role of observation within the Early Years Foundation Stage.

The field of early years care and education has seen radical changes in the last decade. A large number of policies, reforms, initiatives and acts have been introduced with the aim of improving quality and to increase the standards of care and education. The implementation of the Every Child Matters Green Paper (DfES, 2003) and the subsequent Children Act of 2004 brought about changes within the early years. The introduction of a national framework – The Early Years Foundation Stage – was implemented in September 2008. Similarly, the workforce in the early years has seen changes, with the aims of raising quality and training among people working in the sector.

The introduction of the Early Years Professional Status (a *status*, not *qualification*) was seen as the *gold standard* (HM Government, 2006a) which would raise standards in workforce training, in an attempt to meet the quality requirements of the EYFS. The Common Assessment Framework (CAF) – a multi-professional approach to integrate services across the children's and young people's sector – was implemented in April 2006. The Common Assessment Framework was developed with the intention of understanding children's needs at an earlier stage, so that joined-up support could be offered to children, bringing together families alongside the early years workforce and other agencies, such as social services and health visitors.

The aim of this introductory chapter is to consider the key current policy drivers and to highlight the role of observation and assessments within this changing context.

ACTIVITY

Before you start reading this chapter, reflect on your own experiences of early years education. Think back to your own childhood: can you remember what early years provision you experienced? If so, what do you remember about these experiences?

ACTIVITY *continued*

Think about:

1. *The physical environment and the types of activities that you were involved in.*

2. *How many other children there were.*

3. *What you gained from attending an early years setting – what the adults were trying to achieve with you.*

Policy context

The United Nations Convention on the Rights of the Child (UNCRC), adopted by the United Nations General Assembly in 1989, brought about changes in terms of policy making and their implementation for children. The UNCRC is an agreement between the United Nations and the individual countries belonging to it that have chosen to ratify the Convention. Central to this is the recognition that all children have the right and access to education, which should be free, and the UN nations involved are responsible for providing this. It also recognises diversity among children and the issue of equal opportunities, no matter the socio-economic, political or racial group to which each child belongs.

Countries which have ratified the UNCRC have made a commitment to deliver these rights and to incorporate them into their policies for children. The Convention has had a great impact on services and policies for children at a national and international level.

The UK ratified the Convention on 16 December 1991 and it came into force on 15 January 1992.

New Labour policy (1997–2010) focused on minimising poverty and eliminating social disadvantage by supporting families and young children and by increasing the quality of care and education. Miller and Havey (2012), reviewing the policy, conclude that the Labour Government aimed to shape early years policy under four themes: reducing child poverty, evidence-based policy, supporting parents and parenting and ensuring maximum support for the most disadvantaged. All the consequent initiatives and policies introduced by the Labour Government aimed to address these four key issues. A high priority in the agenda of the Labour Government was to eliminate child poverty and to increase the protection of children. This led to the *Every Child Matters* (DfES, 2003) Green Paper and the subsequent Children Act of 2004.

Within Every Child Matters (ECM), it is expected that a number of services will work together to meet five outcomes:

- be healthy;
- be safe;
- enjoy and achieve;

- make a positive contribution;

- achieve economic well-being.

Central to the *Every Child Matters* and *Youth Matters* papers is the protection of children and the prevention of risk and mishaps. The Common Assessment Framework, the notion of the 'lead professional', and the sharing of information have all been developed in an attempt to become useful tools within the children's workforce for meeting the outcomes of Every Child Matters.

Multi-agency or inter-agency working with children and families was key to high quality and effective early years practice. The Common Assessment Framework encourages multi-agency work. A number of different services are asked to communicate with each other to identify additional children's needs not covered by any other service at an early stage, and to provide support and intervention for children and their families. The Common Assessment Framework for children and young people (CAF) is one of the elements in the delivery of integrated, frontline services. It is aimed at sharing assessment information about a child across all children's services and local authority areas, in an attempt to identify early any needs a child might have and to ensure that these needs are met. CAF consists of:

- a shared process to enable practitioners to undertake a common assessment – and then act on the result;

- a standard form to record the assessment;

- a pre-assessment checklist to help decide who would benefit from a common assessment.

It is expected that people in the children's workforce should understand the ECM outcomes, have knowledge of the CAF and be able to effectively complete a CAF checklist. Individual organisations offering services for children are responsible for having at least one member of staff trained to meet the CAF requirements and procedures.

Under the CAF, there are three main procedures. Firstly, there is a need to check whether there is already an assessment for a child, and if not, to prepare to undertake one. Secondly, this assessment could be carried out to identify any appropriate support – for example, liaising with other services to plan a common approach to address problems. Finally, in the spirit of partnerships with parents, asking them to participate in the assessment if, or when, any concerns are raised.
There are important aspects of the implementation of the CAF.

- Gathering information: an important tool in gathering information is observation, especially when young children are involved. There are pre-set assessment checklists available for practitioners to use. These are mostly related to children's development.

- Sharing information: once an assessment has taken place the records should be kept safe and confidential, and yet also accessible, in order to enable children and families to address their needs in an appropriate way and to share these records with the appropriate services.

- The role of the lead professional is to ensure that information is gathered, to liaise with all relevant services and to plan any appropriate action if it is required. Fundamental skills for the lead professional are the ability to understand systematic observations and to record and share findings.

The Labour Government intended to move towards integrated services, whereby a number of professionals from different areas would work together for effective practice with children. On 1 October 2006 the Children's Workforce Development Council (CWDC) became responsible for the implementation of the CAF. Among its duties was to ensure that all children's services were acquiring common skills and knowledge, as the goal is to bring all professionals from different sectors together in order to meet the five outcomes of the ECM.

The CWDC vision is of an early years workforce that:

- supports integrated and coherent services for children, young people and families;
- remains stable and appropriately staffed, whilst exhibiting flexibility and responsiveness;
- is trusted and accountable, and thereby valued;
- demonstrates a high level of skills, productivity and effectiveness;
- exhibits strong leadership, management and supervision.

(CWDC, 2011)

In 2011, CWDC published *Early Years Workforce – The Way Forward* which sets the vision and includes key messages and recommendations to the DfE, the Teaching Agency and to other sector leaders who will support the Early Education and Childcare workforce in the future. In November 2010, the Government announced that they would withdraw the funding from CWDC and, from 1 April 2012, the CWDC would become part of the Teaching Agency.

The impact of a range of policies, reforms and initiatives regarding the early years workforce has led to changes in qualifications and training within the sector. Traditionally, the early years workforce was made up of people entering with a variety of qualifications, backgrounds and experiences. The demands of the policies as well as the implementation of the EYFS are for professionals to work together. The aim is to raise quality standards within the early years, and has led to the creation of a new professional role in the sector. The Children's Workforce Development Council, in an attempt to meet the EYFS requirements, introduced a set of standards and invested in the creation of a new graduate role – the Early Years Professional Status. This is seen as the 'gold' standard, which attempts to ensure the implementation of EYFS and to improve quality by meeting the outlined outcomes. Ofsted, the government body responsible for the inspection of the education sector and the maintenance of standards, would be introduced into the early years sector, meaning that the outcomes each child should meet needed to be measurable.

The creation of the Early Years Professional role includes responsibilities to lead the practice across the EYFS in a range of settings. The Local Authority is the main body responsible for administrating this process. In order to achieve EYPS, candidates need to meet 39 standards and to cover a range of skills. It is now recognised that the Early Years Professional Status is a standardised national training for people who work in the sector. Although it is equivalent to a teacher's qualification, it does not have teaching status.

The Coalition Government has announced an independent review, led by Professor Cathy Nutbrown, to consider how best to strengthen qualifications and career pathways in the early years education. In March 2012 the interim report on early years workforce qualifications was published. The report recommends that it is important to develop courses that prepare people for working in the early years, giving them the right skills in literacy and numeracy and in-depth, up-to-date knowledge of child development. Cathy Nutbrown also suggests that the role of teachers needs to be expanded creating new teaching pathways with an early years specialism, linking the formal education with the early years (Nutbrown, 2012). The early years sector is yet again to see changes. Qualifications are reviewed in the hope that they will improve quality in the sector and positive outcomes in young children's lives.

The Early Years Foundation Stage

The introduction and implementation of The Early Years Foundation Stage (EYFS) as a single quality framework became a reality in September 2008. Before its implementation, the quality framework was determined by three different documents: the *Curriculum Guidance for the Foundation Stage*, the *Full Day Care National Standards for under 8s day care and child minders* and the *Birth to Three Matters* framework papers (DfES, 2007). The EYFS aimed to bring these three documents together into one cohesive framework. The overall aim of the EYFS is to incorporate the five outcomes of the ECM (DfES, 2007).

The EYFS aimed to become an integrated approach to care and education for children, from birth to the end of the Foundation Stage. It emphasises the importance of play and it attempts to help practitioners to plan care and learning appropriate for each child at each stage of his or her development. It also emphasises outdoor play and asks the providers to revisit their practices in terms of outdoor activities, and to encourage outdoor play on a daily basis (DCSF, 2008a).

It also aims to:

- strengthen the links between Birth to Three Matters and the Foundation Stage;

- incorporate elements of the National Standards;

- ensure a consistent approach to care, learning and development from birth to the end of the Foundation Stage.

(DCSF, 2008a)

The intention of The EYFS is to achieve these aims by a principled approach to:

• setting standards;

• promoting equality of opportunity;

• creating a framework for partnership working;

• improving quality and consistency;

• laying a secure foundation for future learning and development.

(DCSF, 2008a)

The introduction of the EYFS has raised the need for training in order to meet its requirements. Section 13 of the Childcare Act (2006) requires local authorities to secure the provision of information and to provide training, to therefore support the early years workforce within the requirements of the EYFS. The EYFS is centralised and provides a single quality framework for early years practice. The training and implementation, however, is devolved at a local level. Local authorities are required to develop action plans based on local needs and priorities.

In 2010 the new Coalition Government commissioned a number of reviews to be undertaken in the policies related to early years. This resulted in the publication of the following: Frank Field's (November 2010) review *The Foundation Years Parenting: Poor Children Becoming Poor Adults*, examining poverty in England and ways to support poor families to get out of a cycle of social deprivation; Graham Allen's (2011) *Early Intervention: The Next Steps*; and Michael Marmot's (2011) *Fair Society, Healthy Lives* and *The Munro Review of Child Protection Report* (2011). All these reviews dealt with key issues of poverty and how deprived families can be supported in order to change their lives. Finally in May 2011, Dame Tickell's review was published, *The Early Years Foundation: Foundations for Life, Health and Learning.* This review aimed to examine the implementation of Early Years Foundation Stage and how it can be improved for raising quality in the early years sector.

Common themes in all these reports were the emphasis on early intervention and protection of children, as well as the elimination of poverty. The Tickell review examined the EYFS in detail, and proposed changes in the learning and development goals and most importantly in the assessment within EYFS. It suggested a decrease in the proposed assessment scales and a more flexible assessment profile for each child. As a result of the Tickell review, in March 2012 the revised EYFS was published by the Department of Education. This consists of two documents: *Statutory Framework for the Early Years Foundation Stage: Setting the Standards for Learning, Development and Care from birth to five* (DfE, 2012a) and *Development Matters in the Early Years Foundation Stage* (non-statutory guidance) (DfE, 2012b). The overarching principles that should shape early years settings remain the same: emphasis on the unique child, positive relationships, enabling environments and children's development and learning areas. These areas comprise: communication and language; physical development; personal, social and emotional development. *Specific* areas include: literacy, mathematics, understanding the world, and expressive arts and design (DfE, 2012a, pages 4–5). In the revised EYFS there is emphasis on three key elements of effective teaching and learning:

- *playing and exploring* – so that children investigate and experience things, and 'have a go';

- *active learning* – so children concentrate and keep on trying if they encounter difficulties, and enjoy achievements;

- *creating and thinking critically* – so children have and develop their own ideas, make links between ideas, and develop strategies for doing things.

(DfE, 2012a, page 7)

Assessment remains an important aspect of the revised EYFS. It is suggested in the *Development Matters in the Early Years Foundation Stage* (DfE, 2012b, page 3) that formative assessment is the *heart of effective early years practice* and that observations is the starting point for assessment and planning for children's learning and development.

The role of observation in the Early Years Foundation Stage

As already indicated, the overall aim of the EYFS is to help practitioners and professionals meet the five outcomes of ECM. The EYFS creates a framework for parents and professionals to work together. Central to ECM is the CAF, which promotes a holistic approach to the assessment of children and which strengthens partnerships between children's services and parents. Moreover, the Common Core of Skills and Knowledge (CWDC, 2007b) is of great importance in order to create a children's workforce which will be able to 'join up' to deliver the five outcomes of the ECM. Under the second heading of the Common Core skills, 'Child and Young Person', the first heading is 'Observation and Judgement'. Professionals in the early years sector should be able to observe, record, analyse and, document children's behaviour, understand their contexts, be sensitive to their needs and be proactive if they observe any unexpected changes in children's behaviour.

There is a statutory requirement for practitioners working in the children's sector for observation. On the one hand there is the CAF as a tool to assess children at an early stage, to help identify additional needs and to try to prevent something from going wrong.

On the other hand, in the early years within the EYFS, assessment is not only important but statutory. The Early Years Foundation Stage Profile (EYFSP) records each child's development and learning needs at the end of the EYFS. It is developed around the key Early Learning Goals of the EYFS and it is based on observations and assessments of each child's achievements, interests and learning styles. It is clearly stated that *the Profile must reflect: ongoing observations; all relevant records held by the setting; discussions with parents and carers and any other adults whom the teacher, parent or carer judges can offer a useful contribution* (DfE, 2012a, page 11).

Among the main roles and responsibilities of the early years professional (normally an EYP) is the ability to act in cases where the CAF is implemented, and thus be able to complete the assessment scales through constant observation of children, communicating these assessment profiles with parents and with local authorities (DfE, 2012a).

It is evident that at policy level there is an emphasis on the ability of the early years workforce to demonstrate observation skills. Early years workforce more than ever now has training to ensure that this skill is mastered and the assessment process understood. Subsequently, this book aims to discuss observation in order to assist the early years workforce to develop a theoretical as well as a practical understanding of systematic ways of observing young children and of recording, analysing and documenting the data obtained.

About this book

In the context of the changes in the early years sector and its workforce, systematic observations and assessments play an important role within the portfolio of skills. This book discusses the role of observation in the early years environment as a tool for assessment for professionals, in relation to current policies and initiatives. The skill of observation is very important to all people working with children. This has been recognised strongly in all the recent policy changes and reflected in the Common Core Skills and the Standards of the EYP. The observation process is not isolated from the rest of your practice or from the educational programme as a whole. It should be integral to it, helping you develop your practice and your understanding of it. This book aims to help you further your understanding of what observation is.

This introductory chapter offers an overview of current policies and the context in which you will work. It aims to examine the importance of observation within the Early Years Foundation Stage Profile which is based on early childhood practitioners' observations and assessments.

Chapter 1 aims to discuss the key influences on early years pedagogy. It reviews the dominant constructions of childhood, philosophical and psychological views which influence our pedagogy and practice in the early years. It also highlights key aspects of learning in early childhood.

Chapter 2 investigates the nature of observation in early years and discusses the role of observation in relation to current legislation and the everyday practice of an early years setting.

Chapter 3 presents the commonly used observation techniques, with some practical examples for you to consider. It explains the three main observation methods – structured, semi-structured and unstructured – illustrating their key advantages and disadvantages.

Chapter 4 deals with the key issues of analysis and documentation of observations. It offers a number of examples from research and different curricular approaches for you to explore and various ways of documenting observations. Finally, it discusses the key limitations of observations.

Chapter 5 addresses the ethics of the observation process in relation to the documentation of your findings, as an integral part of ethical procedures and considerations. How you document your information and with whom you share it is directed by regulations and informs good practice.

Having built a theoretical understanding of the observations, Chapter 6 looks at some practical examples for observing children that focus on their development.

Chapter 7 attempts to discuss observation as a research tool. It examines observation as a qualitative and a quantitative tool and addresses differences between observation for research and observation for practice.

Chapter 8 revisits the discussion on pedagogy and discusses the differences between pedagogy and curriculum. It discusses a curriculum for early years with emphasis on observations, offering three examples from the EYFS, Reggio Emilia and Te Whaariki schemes.

Finally, in the light of a good understanding of the observation process, the final chapter discusses the role of the early years workforce, and draws conclusions as to the importance of observation skills for early years practice.

FURTHER READING

For more information on early years policy:

Anning, A and Ball, M (2008) *Improving Services for Young Children.* London: SAGE

Baldock, P, Fitzgerald, D and Kay, J (2009) *Understanding Early Years Policy (2nd ed.).* London: SAGE.

Fitzgerald, D and Kay, J (2008) *Working Together in Children's Services.* London: Routledge.

Miller, L and Hevey, D (2012) *Policy Issues in the Early Years.* London: SAGE.

Nurse, A (2007) *The New Early Years Professional.* London: Routledge

Simon, CA and Ward, S (2010) *Does Every Child Matter? Understanding New Labour's Social Reforms.* London: Routledge.

To access the revised EYFS visit the following link: **www.foundationyears.org.uk** (Accessed April 17 2012.

1   The pedagogy of early years

Through reading this chapter, you should be able to consider:

- the child in context and how this influences early years pedagogy;

- key philosophical ideas and their impact on pedagogy;

- key developmental theories and how they impact on early childhood pedagogy;

- the differences between pedagogy and curriculum and to examine three curriculum practices: Early Years Foundation Stage; Reggio Emilia; and Te Whaariki – in order for you to be able to reflect on your own practice.

Research into the literature on pedagogy shows that the term is a complex one and extends beyond the narrow approaches of teaching and learning.

Introduction: Towards a discussion on pedagogy

The aim of this chapter is to highlight a number of issues and factors that impact on pedagogy in early childhood education. Any discussion about the nature of pedagogy is a complex one; it is a term which is difficult to define and writers have offered a variety of different definitions and explanations about pedagogy, depending on the context, the policy, classroom teaching and practice, teaching styles and learning styles.

The term pedagogy is used broadly to describe a

> *discipline [that] extends to the consideration of the development of health and bodily fitness, social and moral welfare, ethics and aesthetics, as well as to the institutional forms that serve to facilitate society's and the individual's pedagogic aims.*
>
> (Marton and Booth, 1997, page 178)

Watkins and Mortimore (1999) argue that parsimonious definitions of pedagogy as 'the science of teaching' are fragmented as they lead to a *scientific* approach with formulation of laws and technical approaches, neglecting the views of pedagogy as a body of knowledge that acknowledges the *uncertainty, relativity, complexity and chaos and recognising the role of creativity and social construction in knowledge – creation* (Watkins and Mortimore, 1999, page 2). Instead it is suggested that pedagogy is *any conscious activity by one person designed to enhance learning in another* (Watkins and Mortimore, 1999, page 8).They move on to suggest that pedagogy is underpinned by complexity which:

specifies relations between its elements: the teacher, the classroom or other content, the view of learning and learning about learning. Such a model draws attention to the creation of learning communities in which knowledge is actively co-constructed and in which the focus of learning is sometimes learning itself.

(Watkins and Mortimore, 1999, page 8)

In the twenty-first century, learning environments have changed and they are now concerned not only with teachers but with the learners. They are also concerned with families, policy reforms and a number of other services such as health, social work and local and national global issues: the ecology of the community (Male and Palaiologou, 2012).

Effective education settings are those which have developed productive and synergistic relationships between learners, families, the team and the community, because the context, the locality and the culture in which learners live are vitally important.

(Male and Palaiologou, 2012, page 112)

In other words, pedagogy no longer occurs in isolation or solely in educational environments; it is part of a wider socio-economic, political, philosophical, psychological and educational dialogue. Consequently, you need to seek an in-depth understanding of these relationships in order to be able to discuss what the pedagogy of early years is. However, there is a need to acknowledge that this dialogue will never be complete, *stable and finalised; there is no final point of permanent and perfect equilibrium* (Dahlberg and Moss, 2010, page xix) in any discussion about pedagogy. Seeking standardised, finalised theoretical models of pedagogy might entail the danger of limiting practice rather than developing practices which expound alternative ways of doing things with children and to the enrichment of early years pedagogy.

It is therefore relevant to this chapter to engage views from socio-constructions of childhood, philosophical and psychological ideas in order to gain a broader understanding of those factors which influence pedagogy.

Engaging socio-constructions of childhood in pedagogy

In recent years, research in the field of child development has become increasingly concerned with applying its vast knowledge base to the educational environment and in creating a pedagogy for children. Now we know much more than ever about the family, the school and the community contexts that foster the development of physically, emotionally and socially healthy, cognitively-competent children. More than ever before children are actively involved in the decision-making processes and assessments that influence their lives and experiences.

The way societies perceive childhood impacts upon our approaches to and views of children. The early years policy services and curricula reflect current perspectives of the child within society and therefore inform our pedagogy, as mentioned above. Examining the social construction of childhood, there is a plethora of different readings about children that influence early years practice. Benton (1996), looking at how children are portrayed within the arts and in literature, describes seven types of child:

- the polite child;
- the impolite child;
- the innocent child;
- the sinful child;
- the authentic child;
- the sanitised child;
- the holy child.

David (1993) discusses the work of Dahlberg (1991), who argued that the ways in which different societies define their concept of childhood overlay physiological constraints with their own concepts – or models – of how children should be at certain stages of their lives. David (1993) distinguishes two views: the *child-as-being* view, where children are left to *be children*, and the *child-as-project*, where their lives are mapped out for them.

She comments that both views leave children at a loss; on the one hand, children are not prepared for the expectations of school and society and on the other they are under pressure to achieve (David, 1993). These two views appear to be meaningful in our society, a society that demands from children so many skills, especially during schooling, and also later when approaching adult life.

Hendrick (1997), examining the social constructions of childhood in Britain since the end of eighteenth century, suggests nine views of childhood, reflecting the socio-economic, theological, political and historical changes within British society:

- the natural child;
- the romantic child;
- the evangelical child;
- the child as child;
- the schooled child;
- the 'child-study' child;
- children of the nation;
- the psychological child;
- the child of the welfare state.

Finally, Mills and Mills (2000), in a more recent review of the literature on perspectives of childhood, suggest that there are several more possible views of childhood.

- *Children as innocent* – representing the theological construct that children are a force for good and that there is a need to protect them.

- *Children as apprentice* – concerning children's need for training in order to achieve adulthood (they are viewed as potential adults).

- *Children as persons in their own right* – mainly a view that emerged from the United Nations Convention on Children's Rights (UNCRC, 1989). It is about children as people with rights and responsibilities. Within this view *children can be viewed as fully social beings, capable of acting in the social world and of creating and sustaining their own culture* (Waksler, 1991, page 23).

- *Children as members of a distinct group* – a similar view to children as persons in their own right (which was first established by the United Nations): The child, for the full and harmonious development of his personality, needs love and understanding. He shall, wherever possible, grow up in the care and under the responsibility of his parents, and in any case in an atmosphere of affection and moral and material security; a child of tender years shall not, save in exceptional circumstances, be separated from his mother. (United Nations, 1959, page 198). This view has been embraced by modern literature (Alderson, 2000, 2004; Clark 2005a, 2005b; Dockett and Perry, 2003, 2005; Farell, 2005; Christensen and James, 2008; Harcourt, Perry and Waller, 2011; Bloch, 1992; James and Prout, 1997; Kjorholt, 2001, 2002; Prout, 2000, 2003; Rinaldi, 2005; Clark et al., 2005).

- *Children as vulnerable* – as children are more vulnerable to playground bullying, domestic violence, sexual abuse, consumerist advertising, exploitations of childlike innocence and racial harassment.

- *Children as animals* – a view that relates to the biological development of children and which accepts that, as all animals go through biological development before they are fully mature, so the same happens to children.

They emphasise that *in reality they [the views of children] cannot be isolated* [from each other] *but they are interlinked and overlapping* (page 9). As a result, all these socio constructions of childhood are found to underpin the same social group and to influence the way society and policies are representing these views in terms of curricular practices, policies, services and provisions.

From the above review of the literature, it is hardly surprising that the term pedagogy portrays a relationship between social views and educational practice. As Davies suggests, *pedagogy involves a vision (theory or set of beliefs) about society, human nature, knowledge and production, in relation to educational ends, with terms and rules inserted as to the practical means of their realisation* (1994, page 26).

In the following paragraphs, an overview of the dominant perspectives of childhood is presented, to help you reflect on your own views of childhood which might in turn influence your views about pedagogy and practice.

The innocent child

The view of the child as innocent, and consequently in need of protection from the evils of society, is a view that was derived from Rousseau's philosophical ideas of childhood and was reinforced by theological considerations. Within this idea, the child is viewed as being in need of protection, and also as representing a force for good. Adults are to take responsibility to ensure that the child is raised outside of the 'evil' influence of society.

Preparing the child for adulthood

This is the view of the child as an apprentice for adulthood, in which the child is being trained in order to be prepared for adult life. Within this view the child is being prepared to become a responsible adult. There is an emphasis on training for the child. Such training might include social skills, communication skills and vocational education.

The socially active child

This is the view of the child as a social person, capable of acting in the social world and of creating and sustaining their own culture. An extended view of this is of the child as a member of a distinct group. This view implies that the child needs a loving and secure environment in order to develop personally, socially and emotionally. When a child grows up in care, for example, then this needs to be in an environment where there are conditions for affection and for moral and material security.

The developmental child

This is the view of the child from a developmental perspective, where he or she passes through stages. For example, psychological stage theories, such as Piagetian stages, or psychoanalytical stages. The field of psychology determines the view of the developmental child where, traditionally education, seeks to further its understanding of children. Moreover, early years education has been based on developmental views of how children learn. An examination of the EYFS and Every Child Matters will reveal that the learning goals reflect these views.

The child in need of protection (or the child as potential victim)

The child is viewed as being in need of protection and vulnerable. In some ways, this reflects an emerging view of the child as a potential victim. An examination of all the current policies regarding safeguarding children shows there is an emphasis on protecting them from harm, keeping them safe and on promoting their well-being. Thus policies and services are in place in case the child needs protection.

The 'modern' child

This view is dominant in Western cultures. Children are seen as socially active citizens and now there is a shift from the non-participant child to one who is a social actor, an individual who enacts agency and is capable of participating in activities involving them. Consequently, listening to children's voices has become an essential aspect of daily life.

This social construct places an emphasis on the 'today' child and children are viewed as individual *human beings, holders of rights, who are actively involved in gaining and enjoying their rights . . . so . . . [children are placed] in the position of 'knower'* (Palaiologou, 2012:1) rather than the *child to be*, contrasting traditional and mainly developmental views that children can achieve targets when they are developmentally ready.

Summary

To summarise, as early years care and education are not isolated from the wider cultural and social context of our views of childhood, the pedagogy of early years is influenced by our views. Policy and curricula are determined by our notions of childhood and reflect these views.

ACTIVITY **1**

Considering the different views of childhood, reflect on your own upbringing and consider which views might have shaped your own education. Share your experiences with your fellow students.

As a professional, which views do you think influence your practice?

Engaging philosophical ideas in pedagogy

The field of education has been influenced by a number of philosophers and thinkers in education (see Theory Focus box). These writers are questioning the purpose of education (why?), the nature of education (what?), the type of education (how?) and the recipients of education (for whom?).

THEORY FOCUS

Influential thinkers in education

Thinkers in education	Key ideas
Johann Heinrich Pestalozzi (1746–1827)	Pestalozzi promoted the idea of social justice and was one of the first thinkers to emphasise education based on psychological methods of instruction. He placed emphasis on spontaneity and self-activity. He believed that children should not be given ready-made answers but should arrive at answers themselves. He promoted the idea of education for the whole child and he developed the 'Pestalozzi method', which is based on balancing three elements – hands, heart and head.
Susan Isaacs (1885–1948)	Heavily influenced by the psycho-analytical school of thought, Isaacs promoted the idea of children's freedom in the classroom – and play as a method of expressing themselves and mastering the world through discovery.

John Dewey (1859–1952)	Dewey promoted the idea that education and learning are social and interactive processes. Consequently, schools were viewed as social institutions through which social reform can and should take place. He also promoted the idea of ownership of the curriculum by learners and that all learners are entitled to be part of their own learning. Key terms in Dewey's work are democracy and ethics. He strongly emphasised the role of education as one of creating a place in which to learn how to live: *to prepare him [the student] for the future life means to give him command of himself; it means so to train him that he will have the full and ready use of all his capacities* (1897, page 6).
Maria Montessori (1870–1952)	Montessori took the view that all children are competent beings, and with the support of the environment (child-sized environment-microcosm), children can be encouraged to achieve maximal potential. Emphasis on *absorbent mind* and critical periods where, with the support of self-correcting *auto-didactic* materials, children from a young age can be helped to achieve their potential.
Ludwig Wittgenstein (1889–1951)	Introduced a new way of thinking in philosophy, opposing the traditional philosophical approaches to dialogue. He was interested in language and how humans use language and experience. He used dialogue as a form of investigation and focused on how to pursue a question, how knowledge is learned and how it should be taught.
Carl Rogers (1902–1987)	Rejected the psycho-analytical approaches and placed the self rather than unconscious drives as a key element in personality formation through self-understanding and self-actualisation. He introduced a phenomenological approach which he called client-centred and then person-centred therapy. His ideas about education were derived from his belief that education should be about self-improvement and self-actualisation.
Ivan Illich (1926–)	Promoted radical humanistic ideals and *consciously secular ideology* as a way of planning and attempting *inventive solutions to social problems* (1970). He viewed education outside formal schooling: *educational function was already emigrating from the schools and [think] that, increasingly, other forms of compulsory learning would be instituted in modern society* (1970, page 70).
Lawrence Kohlberg (1927–1987)	Kohlberg was concerned with moral development and believed it could not be separated from cognitive development. He thought cognitive and moral development developed through levels. Each level divided into three stages.

Jurgen Habermas (1929–)	Proposed a critical theory as an underpinning ideology for education. He introduced a method of ideology critique with four stages. He claimed that although ideology is theoretical, it directly applies to practice. The methodology suggested by his critical theory is action research. He introduced eight principles for teaching techniques and promoted the idea that teachers should take into account and work with and on the experiences that learners encounter in the pedagogical act.
Pierre Bourdieu (1930–)	He promoted the idea of reflexivity in human sciences (epistemic reflexivity) and coined the concept of epistemic individuals. Key concepts in his work are *habitus* (how individuals acquire mental structures which determine their views and behaviours) and social strategies (how individuals engage themselves with beliefs and act upon them).
John White (1934–)	He debated the notion of the aim of education and believed in personal responsibility and autonomy of the learner. He promoted the idea of a curriculum that cultivates learner autonomy.
Henry Giroux (1943–)	Viewed schools as places for cultural production and transformation rather than reproduction of knowledge. He promoted the idea that the role of education is to enable emancipatory citizenship and that pedagogical activity is political activity. In that sense, he claimed that pedagogy is about questioning the nature, content and purpose of schooling. As a result, he coined the term *critical pedagogy* and described principles that underpin it. He viewed educators as transformative intellectuals who raise awareness among their learners and said their teaching and learning activities are political.
Gilles Deleuze (1925–1995)	He promoted the idea of practice theory and that individuals can only change themselves within practice. He believed that in order to make a difference in education, teaching and learning should be collaborative actions which can lead to change. He introduced the term *assemblage* which is a flexible unit of social organisation and depends on learning.
Basil Bernstein (1925–2000)	He did a lot of work on language and social class and introduced the idea of social coding systems in education. He examined the role of social classes in relation to pedagogy and schooling and he concluded that working class children are excluded from formal education as the language used from the curriculum is not possible to be followed by them.

Paulo Freire (1921–1997)	He viewed education as a form of social inclusion and all his life promoted the idea that it should not reverse the reproduction of the forms of exclusion that are mirrored in society. He viewed the teachers' role as important inside but also outside the classroom. He promoted the idea of teachers as agents of ethical and political meanings and he believed that teachers should show respect for their students and their knowledge.
Jean-François Lyatord (1924–1998)	He promoted the idea that the role of education is not to arrive at a unity of agreed knowledge but to celebrate differences, plurality and diversity. He criticised government agendas of *performativity* in education and objected to target/outcome-driven education.
Michel Foucault (1926–1984)	He was concerned with the search of how human beings can develop critical thought to exist as rational beings. He examined the nature of knowledge in relation to education, economy and politics. He contributed to educational thought and provided theoretical and methodological ways to study the field, focusing on the relations of power and knowledge.

Table 1.1   Influential thinkers in education

Thinkers and philosophers have been influential in the way they have viewed education and pedagogy in societies. A key thinker in education and still very influential, Paulo Freire (1970, 1973, 1994, 1998) debates the role of education in societies and claims that education should not reverse the reproduction of the forms of exclusion – political, social, economical, racial – and he claims that:

> the pedagogy of the oppressed [is] a pedagogy which must be forged with, not for, the oppressed (be they individuals or whole peoples) in the incessant struggle to regain humanity. This pedagogy makes oppression and its causes objects of reflection by the oppressed, and from that reflection will come liberation.

(Freire, 1982, page 25)

Extending this view Giroux (2011) introduces the idea of critical pedagogy as a way of responding to deep social problems and objects to the regime of market-, target- and outcome-driven pedagogy. *Reclaiming public and higher education as sites of moral and political practice for which the purpose is both to introduce students to the great reservoir of diverse intellectual ideas and traditions and to engage those inherited bodies of knowledge through critical dialogue, analysis and comprehension* (Giroux, 2011, page 13). He views education and pedagogy as a platform for people to develop a questioning approach to authority.

On this issue Derrida (1992) advocates the idea that the role of education is to test questions:

When the path is clear and given, when certain knowledge opens up the way in advance, the decision is already made, it might as well be said there is none to make: irresponsibility, and in good conscience, one simply applies or implements a programme. Perhaps, and this would be the objection, one never escapes the programme. In that case, one must acknowledge this and stop talking with authority about moral or political responsibility. The condition of possibility of this thing called responsibility is a certain experience and experiment of the possibility of the impossible; the testing of the aporia from which one may invent the only possible invention, the impossible invention.

(Derrida, 1992, page 41, original emphasis)

In Derrida's view, education is about experiencing, trying out real ideas, dealing with authentic problems. He sees this process as the only way to improve ideas thus the impossible invention.

Similarly Bernstein questions the way we approach knowledge in educational settings and how this forms our pedagogy: How a society selects, classifies, distributes, transmits and evaluates the educational knowledge it considers to be public, reflects both the distribution of power and the principles of social control (Bernstein, 1971, page 47). He distinguishes between pedagogy and curriculum: Curriculum defines what counts as valid knowledge, pedagogy defines what counts as the valid transmission of knowledge, and evaluation defines what counts as a valid realisation of knowledge. (Bernstein 1971, page 48). Bernstein also debated the idea of social inequalities in education.

Another approach to pedagogy is the one introduced by Bruner who divides education into three dominant views:

- seeing children as imitative learners: the acquisition of 'know-how' (apprenticeship);

- seeing children as learning from didactic exposure: the acquisition of propositional knowledge;

- seeing children as thinkers: the development of inter-subjective interchange – pedagogy is to help the child understand better, more powerfully, less one-sided.

(Bruner, 1996, pages 53–61)

And on this basis, other thinkers (Isaacs, 1930, 1933, 1935; Lyotard, 1979; White, 1973, 1982, 1990, 1994) have turned their attention to the conflict between pedagogy- and government-driven curricula and they discuss the role of educators and how they should engage in pedagogical activities. For example, Lyotard (1979) argues that educators are frustrated professionals and introduces the terms *telematics*. The idea is that educationalists simply become providers of information concerned with the mechanics of the process instead of the process itself. He opposed the legitimacy of education through *performativity*, driven by targets and assessment based on targets culture, because he believes that the supporters of performativity urge that education should impart only the knowledge and skills necessary to preserve and enhance the operational efficiency of society. He claims that knowledge should not have to have any intrinsic performativity but instead plurality, dissensus innovation, imagination and creativity are the drivers in the quest for pedagogical practices in education. All theorists argue that the goal of educators is the discovery of new ideas and concepts and experiencing these ideas and concepts with the learners.

Summary

To summarise, philosophical thinking has contributed to the discussion of pedagogy by emphasising that pedagogy and education should:

- be based on rigorous research;

- be characterised by critique on inputs (policy, curriculum, pedagogy) and outputs (learning, outcomes);

- not be about the 'one size fits all', conceptual framing of education (Cole, 2011) but should deal with actions justified by the dynamics of the ecology of the community of learning (Palaiologou, 2011);

- be characterised by the responsible exercise of academic judgement;

- not reinforce a distinction between theory and practice but should be concerned with the nature of knowledge and how it is acquired;

- be a powerful enactment of Derrida's notion of *testing aporia (questions)* and seeking the *impossible invention.*

Although all these thinkers discussed the issues in general, one can see the applicability in early childhood pedagogy and education. On the one hand, the early years workforce needs to meet the government agenda (EYFS) which is based on Principles (official approach), Standards (fixed and limited), Learning and developmental goals (developmental approach) and 'Universal' assessment (as a way of measurement, evaluation, inspection) and this has led to reporting 'what to do' rather than actually 'doing'. Practitioners attend extensive training on '*how to do*', putting aside the 'known being' which is the essential element in the construction of effective pedagogy. It is argued that while the current policy context (the EYFS) in which education and care in early childhood is situated is both exciting and challenging, it remains imperative that practitioners rise to the challenge of critically reflecting how they are positioned and how they seek to position themselves and to construct professional identities. In other words, it is important how practitioners themselves will embark upon a search for effective pedagogy.

ACTIVITY **2**

Reflecting on the following quote, in your view, who is the 'wise' practitioner in early childhood?

The wise practitioner is the one who can draw upon and add to a wise set of knowledge, can use that knowledge and professional experience to deliberate about and reflect upon practice, and one who can act wisely within educational situations by relying on a growing and deepening understanding of what it means to teach and be a teacher (Feldman, 1997, page 758).

Engaging psychological theories in pedagogy

As our views of childhood are influenced by historical, philosophical, economical and cultural changes, similarly modern theories of child development have roots extending far into the past. For example, in medieval times children were regarded as miniature adults, a view called *preformationism* (Aries, 1962). According to him, childhood was not a distinct period of life and this can be seen from the fact that children did not have clothes made specifically for them, nor were they provided with toys or given different activities to adults. As soon as children were sufficiently independent they were entering adult life and joining the adult workforce.

By the sixteenth century, childhood was identified as a distinct phase of life. However, the dominant Puritan concept of original sin led to a harsh philosophy when it came to rearing children. There was a need to train the child, in order to help the child to be 'cleansed' of original sin. The Enlightenment brought ideas favouring a more humane treatment of children (Berk, 1997), with an emphasis on children's education. Locke's *tabula rasa* statement of 1892, in which children were viewed as a blank slate that could be educated and shaped in any way that adults wanted, provided the basis for twentieth century behaviourism, whilst Rousseau's (1911) notion of the child as *noble savage* foreshadowed the concepts of stage and maturation.

A century later, Darwin's theory of evolution stimulated a scientific approach to the study of the child. The great revolution in research into child development occurred in the 1930s and 1940s (Dixon and Learner, 1992). Darwin's theory was the origins of the ethnology theory, which is concerned with the adaptive (or survival) value of behaviour (Lorenz and Tinberger, in Dewsberry, 1992).

Child guidance professionals turned to the field of psychology in order to further their understanding of how children develop and learn. The following paragraphs discuss the dominant psychological theories in the field of child development and learning.

Psychoanalytical theory

The psychoanalytical theory is dominated by the work of two main theorists: Sigmund Freud and Erik Erikson. Both are widely read and influence the way that we think about children today.

Sigmund Freud's theory challenged the view of the child as innocent, provoking a debate about children's experiences and how these experiences subsequently shape children's personalities. The main emphasis in Freud's theory was placed on development being driven by aggressive and sexual instincts (Freud, 1923, 1933). He developed a psychosexual theory that formulated different stages of psychosexual development. Freud (1964) believed that sex is the most important instinct in human development. In his view the different activities that a baby does – such as sucking the thumb or a child breaking rules – are activities that relate to the child's psychosexual development. Freud did not view sex in childhood from an erotic perspective. Instead, he believed that when children develop and move through different stages, the focus of the sex instinct is moving in different parts of their bodies. Thus Freud's *stages* are related to parts of the human body.

He suggested that children move through five psychosexual stages during which three components of personality are developed: the *id*, *ego*, and *superego*. When babies are born the *id* is already present and it helps the new-born to satisfy basic biological needs. For example, when a baby is hungry, he or she cries for food. The ego is related to consciousness and reflects the child's ability to learn, reason and remember. When a baby is hungry, for example, he or she can remember how to receive food and waits for his or her bottle. The final component of personality is the *superego* and this starts developing between two-and-a-half and three years of age. The *superego* is related to moral values and is the internalisation of these moral values and received rules (Freud, 1933).

Erik Erikson was a Freudian student who did not agree with Freud's emphasis on the sexual instinct. He modified Freud's theory by also taking into consideration the environment that children grow up in. Erikson (1963, 1982) introduced the idea of cultural and social influences upon human development. He suggested that children must cope with *social realities* in order to develop appropriate patterns of behaviour. Erikson placed an important role on the social environment and hence suggested his own eight stages of psychosocial development. He believed (1963) that human beings develop through eight *crises* (or psychosocial stages) during their lives. Each of these stages is related to biological development and to social and cultural interactions at certain times of our lives.

Both Freud and Erikson offered us a detailed account of children's personal, social and emotional development. In the field of developmental psychology the psychoanalytical theory was criticised as limited, in terms of suitably explaining a child's development and learning comprehensively. Although both theorists had a significant influence on the study of children's development (Tyson and Taylor, 1990), they do not offer us an adequate explanation of *how* and *why* this development takes place (Shaffer and Kipp, 2007).

Psychoanalysis and observation

Observation in psychoanalysis is central and it can safely be said that within this field of psychology the observation of infants was first introduced as a result of the pioneering work of Bick (1964) in the field of observation study, especially infant observation in family contexts. Bick proposed in *Notes on Infant Observation in Psycho-analytic Training* (1964) that observations of infants should be integrated into the curriculum for young children as a tool for enabling us to understand infant development. Psychoanalysis has introduced precise observation techniques to be used in family contexts. Observers work in the natural environment of the family where they find a space to enable them to experience the interactions between infants and families without participating in any action. Afterwards, observers write the notes in a form of report that conveys their understanding of what has been observed. The field of psychoanalysis has offered us observation techniques in naturalistic environments and infant observation techniques are now widely used in early years settings.

Behaviourism

Behaviourism changed ways of thinking in developmental psychology. The behaviouristic school of psychology placed much emphasis on observations. Theorists within the school of behaviourism – such as Watson, Pavlov and Skinner, who formed the main ideas of this theory – developed more scientific ways of observing in order to understand development.

The main principles of behaviourism can be summarised by the following:

- human behaviour, especially social behaviour, is acquired rather than inborn;

- emphasis on the role of environmental stimuli;

- a focus on learning. Learning is defined as changes in behaviour which occur as the result of experience and interactions with the environment.

(Glassman, 2000)

This theory offers a detailed account of how human beings learn. It has contributed to furthering our understanding of children's development and learning and has offered a scientific approach to the observation of children.

However, it does not consider the social and cultural context of human beings. One theorist who criticised behaviourism for taking little account of the cognitive and socio-cultural factors that influence human development was Bandura, who proposed a social learning theory as an alternative.

Behaviourism and observation

Observation has been central to behaviourism. Behaviourists are concerned with behaviours worthy of study, that is, those which can be observed directly. Thus they have added to observation the elements of measurements and repetition of observation so that, from the same findings, other conclusions can be drawn. They have also offered a quantifying approach to observation. They have contributed to controlled non-participant observation where behaviours are observed, not in naturalistic environments, but in controlled conditions such as laboratory settings. Behaviouristic observation of humans led behaviourists to suggest that human responses to situations were almost predictable, via trial and error and via the principle of what would be the most profitable, least painful or best for the individual, and that thus, training could shape an individual. This implied the elimination of free will from the individual and the wider socio-cultural environment that individuals live in.

Attachment theory

In early childhood education one of the most influential ideas in forming relationships with young children is attachment theory.

There are two psychological theories that discussed attachment. The first one comes from behaviourism (Dollard and Miller, 1950) who suggest, in line with behaviouristic ideas, that attachment is a learned behaviour. Babies learn to associate the person who feeds them, cleans them and looks after them (mainly the mother, or the primary carer) with a feeling of comfort. Thus a bond is developed with the primary carer through classical conditioning. So every time babies see the primary carer, they feel comfortable. A number of behaviours such as crying and smiling bring desirable behaviours such as breast feeding and social interaction, and through operant conditioning, babies learn to repeat these behaviours to get what they want or need.

The second approach comes from the field of ethology. The pioneering work of Bowlby (1969, 1958) and Ainsworth (1973), define attachment as an emotional bond that is established and develops between one person and another, in particular between babies and their mothers or primary carers. Bowlby (1969, page 194) defines attachment as a *lasting psychological connectedness between human beings*. After researching babies and their relationships with their primary carers, he suggested that the primary carer (usually the mother) provides safety and security to the baby. Babies need that dual relationship in order to survive and develop. Prior work by Lorenz (1935) and Harlow and Zimmermann (1958), based on observations of animal ethology, have demonstrated similar patterns of behaviour with animals. Bowlby extended his work to human beings. He suggested that a child forms one primary attachment (monotropy) and that attachment-person becomes a secure basis for the child for developing and exploring the world. He also believed that the attachment relationship becomes a model for all future relationships.

Ainsworth extended Bowlby's theory and after a number of observations she claimed that attachment is developed in stages. Attachment theory has offered us an insight into children's development and has become influential in the early years setting. An extensive approach to attachment is the key person in the early years settings (Palaiologou 2010).

THEORY FOCUS

John Bowlby's stages in the development of attachment

Approximate age (months)	Stage	Description
0 to 2 and over	Orientation to signals without discrimination of human figure	The infant shows orientation to social stimuli – grasping, reaching, smiling and babbling. The baby will cease to cry when picked up or when seeing a face. These behaviours increase when the baby is in proximity to a companion, although the baby cannot distinguish one person from another.
1 to 6 and over	Orientation to signals directed towards one or more discriminated human figures (mainly human faces)	Similar orientation behaviours as in the first stage appear, but they are markedly directed to the primary care-giver. Evidence of discrimination begins at one month for auditory and at two and a half months for visual stimuli.

6 to 30 and over	Maintenance of proximity to discriminated human figure by means of locomotion as well as signals	The repertoire of responses to people increases to include following a departed mother, greeting her on return and using her as a base for exploration. Strangers are treated with caution and may evoke alarm and withdrawal; others may be selected as additional attachment figures (for example fathers).
24 to 48 and over	Formation of a goal-corrected partnership	The child begins to acquire insight into the mother's (or primary carer's) feelings and goals, which lead to co-operative interaction and partnership.

(Bowlby, J (1969) *Attachment*, New York: Basic)

Table 1.2   John Bowlby's stages in the development of attachment

Attachment and observation

Extensive naturalistic observation, as well as controlled observation, has been used by the field of ethology. Bowlby and his followers drew on the field of ethology to develop their own approach to observations. They also borrowed the infant observation technique from the psychoanalytical field and offered research rigour from their scientific field. Whereas psychoanalytical infant observation was not intrusive, Bowlby and his followers (see Ainsworth 1973, 1979, 1969, 1985, 1989; Winnicott 1986, 1987, 1995, 2005) added an intrusive observation procedure in infant observation. Intrusive observation is concerned with reactions of children where a change is occurring. It takes place in a controlled environment (see Ainsworth's experiments with babies and their mothers). The focus is to investigate the pattern of behaviour that will occur if the routine of the baby is disturbed.

Social cognition

Albert Bandura (1971, 1977, 1986, 1989, 2001) argued that human beings develop by using their cognitive abilities in the social and cultural environment in which they live. He suggested the idea of observational learning as an important aspect of development: human beings develop and learn by the examples of others. Children make sense of the world and learn how to behave in particular moments of their lives through observing others (e.g. parents, teachers and other children). Bandura elaborates this idea with examples of children being violent. He presented to young children, in a controlled laboratory setting, an adult beating a doll. The children were then invited to go into a room and play with this doll and with other toys that were there. Observing children's responses, he demonstrated that children imitated what the adult did and that they bit the doll. Bandura concluded that children continuously learn behaviours through the observation of others.

Although Bandura studied development as part of the environment, he did not merely provide a limited description of the environment as an influential factor in human development.

Social cognition and observation

Similar to behaviourism, social cognition has been based heavily on observations but, whereas behaviourism has introduced controlled observations in a laboratory context, social cognition moved beyond this and employed psychoanalytical methods using naturalistic observations. For social cognition, observation of others is seen as a way for people to learn and to develop an understanding of the environment. Knowledge is acquired directly via observations.

Ecology

In contrast to Bandura, Urie Bronfenbrenner (1977, 1979, 1989, 1995, 2005), the originator of ecological systems theory, viewed the natural environment as the most influential factor in human development. He challenged theorists who study human development and learning in artificial and laboratory contexts and proposed the study of human development within the natural environment. He defined an *environment* as being *a set of nested structures, each inside the next, like a set of Russian dolls* (1979, page 22). As a result, he viewed the child as developing within a complex system of relationships, affected by the multiple levels of the surrounding environment, such as immediate settings within broad cultural values, laws and customs. His main idea of how children develop within systems is illustrated in the following figure:

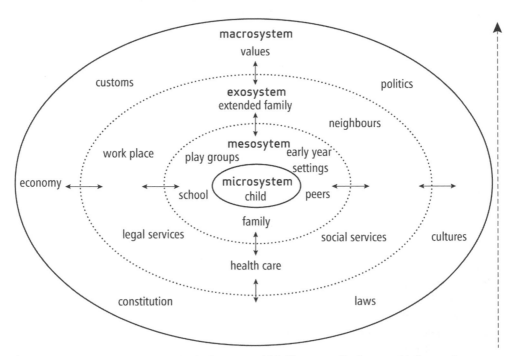

Figure 1.1   Bronfenbrenner's ecological system which illustrates the layers of influence in a child's life

As Figure 1.1 illustrates, *the nested structures* are systems:

- microsystem (the closest environment of the child such as parents and grandparents, family friends);

- mesosystem (the immediate environment that relates to family such as neighbourhood, school);

- exosystem (the different settings that might influence a child's development, such as parents' working environments, cultural groups, religious groups to which parents belong);

- macrosystem (the wider socio-economic, political, cultural and legal contexts).

For Bronfenbrenner, human development involves interactions of these four systems – the micro-, meso-, exo- and macro-systems – over time. This approach to child development emphasises children as active participants in creating their own environments and their experiences of their interactions with their social context as important aspects of human development.

Ecology and observation

Ecological approaches use mainly naturalistic observations. They are concerned with direct observation of behaviour in multiple settings such as home, school, social activities in all four systems – micro, meso, exo and macro – in order to have a complete picture of the person's social development. They are also concerned with direct observation of more than one person – multi-person systems in the same place as a way of examining interactions among people.

Cognition

In developmental psychology the school of cognition has been one of the most dominant theories in child development. Cognition is concerned with the *study of the processes involved in cognition – the processes involved in making sense of the environment and interacting appropriately with it* (Eysenck, 1995, page 10). The mental processes through which we attempt to understand the world were defined as:

- thinking and knowing;

- reasoning;

- learning;

- problem solving;

- using language;

- memory;

- perception.

The two most important theorists who have furthered our understanding of child development in cognitive psychology are Jean Piaget – who emphasised that a child has an active mind inhabited by rich structures of knowledge – and Lev Vygotsky. Vygotsky's socio-cognitive perspectives (1986) focused on how cultural values, beliefs, customs and social interactions are necessary for children in acquiring new ways of thinking.

Piaget

Piaget's theory suggests that children develop through stages. Children develop and construct knowledge (schema) via these stages. According to Piaget (1929, 1952, 1954, 1962, 1968, 1969), the schemata, which are specific psychological structures, change with age. Piaget's cognitive theory suggests that during the first two years of life, cognition can be seen in the baby's motor actions towards the environment.

To explain how children acquire schemata and subsequently change these, Piaget identifies two important intellectual functions: assimilation and accommodation. Assimilation is the process by which the child cognitively adapts to, and organises, the environment, and which therefore allows growth but not a change of schemata. The process responsible for changes in schemata is accommodation. Accommodation is part of the process of adaptation in which old schemata are adjusted and new ones are created to produce a better fit within the environment. The processes of assimilation and accommodation are necessary for cognitive development. For Piaget, these two processes interact in a balanced way and he calls that interaction *equilibrium*. This is a self-regulatory process whose tools are assimilation and accommodation. Children with equilibrium transfer external experiences into internal structures (or 'schemata').

It is not until the end of the second year that children begin to use mental-symbolic processes in order to adapt to their environment (Piaget, 1952). Piaget (1952) made clear that the behaviour of small infants, although not conceptually based, was nevertheless intelligent. By this he meant that infants had ways of meeting their needs, of using their own resources and other resources in the environment, and of adapting those resources to the specific nature of the task at hand. This sensory motor intelligence was embodied not in the mind, but in the actions and movements that the baby made in direct interaction with its environment (Piaget, 1952, 1962). There follows the move into childhood and into pre-operational thought. The distinguishing characteristic between infancy and childhood is the use of language and the ability to perform logical reasoning.

Another characteristic that assists development from infancy to childhood is the *object concept* or the concept of *object permanence*. This refers to a set of implicit, commonsense beliefs that we all share about the basic nature and behaviour of objects, including ourselves. When an object disappears from one's sight, adults do not assume that it has thereby gone out of existence, but this skill does not exist from the beginning of our life and is acquired only gradually. When children acquire object permanence it is then when symbolic representation involves implications for language, attention and for social development.

According to Piaget, knowledge is not absorbed passively from the environment, but is constructed through interactions and experiences between the mental structures (schemata) and the environment. As a result, knowledge is constructed from a child's actions in the environment. In Piaget's theory there are three kinds of knowledge:

- physical;

- logical-mathematical;

- social.

The Piagetian theory has had a great impact on the early years environment. The developmentally appropriate practices in early years settings, and the pedagogical principles that have evolved as a result of his theory, have changed the ways that learning in the early years is viewed.

For example, the physical environment of the classroom has changed within the last few decades. The classroom design itself provides a context for the child, and is now a dominant consideration for an early years class. There is a cultural richness in early years classes, where a wealth of real life experiences is transferred into the environment. There are carpets where children can relax, library areas where children can have their first experiences of reading, corners such as a sand area, construction areas with Lego blocks, post offices, etc. All these areas in an early years classroom help children to experience with materials and learn through experience and interaction with the environment. Such richness of materials in a classroom furthers a child's understanding of the world, and they are the learning opportunities that the early years class is offering to children, in order to construct and facilitate knowledge.

The following description presents a picture of a classroom that fosters development and promotes learning, and is influenced by Piagetian ideas:

CASE STUDY

Example of a physical environment of a classroom which applies Piaget's theories

The classroom is divided into small learning areas, where groups of children may play with sand or occupy themselves in parallel or co-operative play with bricks, Lego, or painting, while others are supported by the early years professional in a group task. Others are engaged in symbolic play or dramatic play. A few children may be at the writing area. One or two are on the floor looking at a big picture book, or sitting in a chair in the library corner looking at or reading books, leading, perhaps, to a shared reading with an educator or a peer.

Outside, children may be involved with larger materials and apparatus in solitary or co-operative imaginative play, or with others in socially-agreed play. Children may be painting at an easel or writing. The early years professionals move between the various activities, supporting children with their experience of the materials. Occasionally, usually at the start or the end of the session, the class comes together for a group story reading, a shared book experience or a song. Thus, a whole range of activities will be taking place supporting children's learning through experience and interactions with materials.

Vygotsky

While Piaget viewed cognitive development as the result of the individual child's interaction with the environment, Vygotsky (1986, 1962) expands further on that view. Vygotsky emphasised the importance of social interaction for children's cognitive development. He introduced the idea of the *zone of proximal development* (or *ZPD*). Vygotsky (1986) identifies *the zone of actual development* which *defines actions that have already matured; that is, the end of product of development.* This refers to a number of skills that a child has already mastered and which help the child to achieve certain tasks. However, during development, children should preferably be placed in the zone of proximal development where the potential development of a child is situated. . . . *[Children] that have not yet matured but are in the process of [acquiring . . .] functions that will mature tomorrow, but are currently in an embryonic state* (Vygotsky, 1986, page 87). This refers to a range of skills that the child cannot yet handle, but with the help of a more mature or skilled peer or an adult, the child can master these skills. In practice, this means that children need social interaction. The help of an adult or of other children is an important and integral part of a child's development.

In Vygotsky's theory there is emphasis on what children *can* do rather than what they *cannot* do. Consequently, learning is constructed as a partnership between the child and the adult.

CASE STUDY

ZPD with the help of an adult

The following example attempts to demonstrate how the interaction of the early years professional with children helps them to read a picture book. The book is about animals. At the end of each page there is some push-button music playing to the sound of the animal illustrated in the picture.

EYP: *Do you want to look at this book with me?*
George: [He just nods his head.]
EYP: *So, do you want to look at the book?*
George: *Yes.*
EYPS: [reads the story] *On the farm the little dog . . .*
[George interrupts the reading and presses a button to listen to the music.]
EYP: *We have not reached the part where you must press the button for the music. Do you want to wait? It is not going to take long.*
[George looks at the EYP and presses the button again.]
EYP: *Do you want me to suggest something to you, then? We can do the following: I will give you the book for you to turn the pages and listen to all the noises, and then, if you want, we can still look at it together.*
[George takes the book and starts to press the button more than three times.]

EYP: *You know, if we turn the page like this you should be able to listen to some more nice sounds. Shall we do it like this?* [Taking the book gently from George's hand and turning the page slowly.]

[George sees the new button and presses it. He presses it about three times and then turns the next page by himself, discovers the button and starts the next piece of music playing.]

After he has experienced the whole book, the EYP asks George if he still wants to look at the book and read it. In this way George discovered that he had to press the buttons in order to listen to the music – the same way in which he learnt how to turn the pages. This happened with some help.

ZPD with the help of a more experienced peer

Another example of ZPD is illustrated in the following extract. In this one it is a mature peer who offers help to another child:

> *Sophia, Raj and Anka were in the library corner with a large number of books. They were looking at the pictures.*

> *The early years professional said that it was tidy-up time, so all three of them started to put the books and the newspapers back in their places, according to the symbols that had been designed to categorize the different types of books and magazines.*

> *Tidiness is not simply the act of shelving books back in the library, but putting them back according to their themes. These were represented by the use of small pictures: the labels bore different symbols for storybooks, knowledge books, fantasy books, talking books, magazines, and so on.*

Storybooks

Talking books

Magazines

Raj: *This is a magazine – it goes with the magazines, next to hairdresser's shop, and this one goes here with the storybooks.*
Anka: *What about this one?*
Sophia: *This is a storybook and goes . . . oh yes . . . here, where the symbol for 'books' is.*
Anka: *Oh! Here's another one* (Anka picks up a Talking Book and puts it in the right place).

To summarise, both Piaget and Vygotsky are important because they challenge educators to rethink children's cognitive development. They further our understanding of how children think, develop and learn, offering us a view that young children are more capable than we perhaps had once assumed. Both theorists placed an emphasis on what children can do, and they viewed learning not only as construction of knowledge, but as an ability to use that knowledge and to apply it appropriately in different contexts. They changed the ways in which we consider children's abilities. Now we can offer a more enriched environment to young children, full of activities and support that enhance their own development and their learning.

Cognition and observation

The field of cognitive psychology employs a number of observation techniques. Observation within the field of cognitive psychology structured and focuses on aspects of development: verbal ability, logical-analytical ability, psychomobility (flexibility of thought), memory (short-term, long-term, working memory recall), analytic-synthetic (ability to create an entity) and psychospatial ability (our ability to perceive environmental patterns). Although they acknowledged that these are not independent from each other and that interaction is necessary, they developed methods to test and observe them separately at an experimental level (Anderson, 1983). In the field of education, the Piagetian tests and systematic observations he has developed have changed methods of study.

ACTIVITY 3

In the following example from an observation in an early years setting, try to investigate whether you can identify any of the ideas of Piaget and Vygotsky in practice.

Activity: Planting beans

The early years professional introduced the activity and the diary to a small group of children. They had to write down who put water on the beans and when, and to chart the beans' development through making drawings. Then, with the assistance of the adults, the children started to fill in the notebook according to their daily observations. Every day the group was asked to spend about five minutes checking the beans, and then to record their observations in the notebook. In the second week after the planting, when the children had finished checking the plants, they went to the writing area and occupied themselves there. When they had finished, they came back to the early years professional. The child in the following extract wanted to write down her name on her drawing, but did not know how, and so she approached the EYP.

C1: Can you write down my name?
EYP: What have you done in your drawing?
C1: I draw what I see in the beans.
EYP: So what do you say, then?
C1: That this bean [points to the big blue shapes similar to a circle on her drawing] has grown so big. Here it is [pointing to her drawing]. I wrote my own letters.

EYP: And what do these letters say?

C1: [As if reading] 'The bean is big'. This is my gardening notebook. Can you write my name?

EYP: What are the sounds of your name?

C1: Lisa.

EYP: What is the first one?

C1: Lisa.

EYP: What is the first one you can hear?

C1: 'L'?

EYP: Yes. Let's write down the letter 'L'.

Comment

During this activity we can see Piaget's idea that children learn actively through interaction with the actual plants (the real world is transferred into the class), and they were able to construct a product/knowledge/schema with real life examples as a context. Children were given roles and responsibilities and through this activity a context was provided for children in order to learn how the plants develop.

In the dialogue with the EYP and the child we can identify the help the EYP offers the child in creating her own notebook and to link sounds to letters.

Within the dialogue above, the zone of proximal development can be identified. The child discusses her request with the early years professional and through the guidance of the adult the child has begun to make sense of letters as symbols.

Summary

The field of child development continues to seek new directions. Information-processing views the development of the mind as a symbol-manipulating system through which information flows (Klahr, 1992). This approach helps researchers to achieve a clear understanding of what children of different ages do when faced with tasks and problems. New technological achievements in the medical field, such as MRI technology, have helped neuroscience to understand how the brain develops and functions. There is more evidence available now to explain how parts of the brain are used when a child faces a task or a problem.

Comparing these child development theories, we can conclude that they differ in many respects. They each focus on different aspects of development but all use observations as their main tool to study children. The psychoanalytical theory emphasises children's social and emotional development. Piaget's cognitive theory, information-processing, and Vygotsky's socio-cultural theory stresses the importance of the social learning environment in children's thinking. They are investigating child development in the context of a non-isolated environment and regard the child as an active learner through experience and interaction with that environment – both early and later experiences are important. The remaining approaches – behaviourism and ecological systems theory – discuss factors assumed to affect all aspects of a child's functioning.

Considering the influence of these theories in the field of early years education and care, they can offer a perspective of the child-as-learner, where learning is determined by the child's own development.

Conditions for learning

Similar to pedagogy, learning is not an activity that occurs in isolation. One of the main principles of the EYFS is to develop an enabling environment for children's learning and development. The early years setting should not be separated from wider cultural and social contexts. Although the early years professional is working with a national quality framework (the EYFS), he or she should look to develop local conditions for learning that apply to the needs of the immediate setting and which take the environment into consideration.

In such a learning environment, certain skills are not developed in isolation. Piaget viewed human development as an integrated process where feelings, emotions and relationships have an effect on cognitive skills, such as on numeracy and literacy. Learning in the early years is the product of many experiences in meaningful contexts.

In designing educational programmes and activities for children the following conditions should be considered:

Emphasis on children's development

The development of a child is central in early years practice. From a cognitive perspective, the key developmental areas are physical, social, emotional and moral development, language, numeracy, thinking, memory, attention, perception and reasoning. These areas are reflected in EYFS as:

Prime areas:

- Communication and language
- Physical development; and
- Personal, social, emotional development

Specific areas:

- literacy;
- mathematics;

- understanding the world; and

- expressive arts and design

(DfE, 2012, pages 4–5)

Emphasis on play

Play is important in early years. Within the EYFS again there is great emphasis on play. The EYFS describes play as *purposeful*. In an attempt to understand this, we need to ask *what exactly is play*?

Moyles (1989) defines play as the situation *when children do their learning*. Play is when children have opportunities to express their thoughts and emotions, to try out new things and possibilities, to put different elements of a situation together in various ways and to look at problems from different viewpoints (Bruner, 1972). An important element of play is pleasure. Children need play to enjoy themselves, as well as to enrich their experiences whilst interacting with their environment. Play for young children should not been seen as a separate activity that children do at a specific time. It is something that very young children, in particular, do constantly. Consequently, play is oriented by spontaneity. Early forms of play in very young children lack any organisation and are used by children to help them make sense of the world, to communicate with others and to explore their environment.

Emphasis on children's needs

Children's needs are important factors that influence their learning. These derive from developmental needs such as physical activities, social and emotional well being and opportunities for play.

ACTIVITY **5**

Can you think of other needs?

Emphasis on children's freedom to choose materials and activities

The importance of children's participation has been emphasised in a number of policies relating to children, such as the *United Nations Rights for the Child* and *Every Child Matters* document. The enabling of children as active learners, who are able to take control of their own learning and development, requires an environment where children are given the appropriate opportunities to participate in choosing their own materials and activities.

Emphasis on children's ownership of their learning

Similarly, children should be given opportunities to explore their own learning. They should not be underestimated in terms of their abilities to translate their interests into activities, and thus to explore the world. Children's internal needs drive them to form relationships with other children and adults, and in forming these relationships they discover new ways of learning.

Pedagogy in practice

Developing a pedagogy for early years requires the construction of a professional identity. Within this process, it is important for the early years professional to have a good understanding of a variety of developmental theories, as well as pedagogical practices, and an understanding of children's developmental needs.

However, the early years professional has to work within a context. Miller *et al* (2003) comparing different curricula across the time line and in other countries, found that *curricula guidance for the early years has become increasingly centralised in a number of countries* (page 113). Again, the early years professional is asked to be able to work creatively and to improve practice in this sector.

This is a difficult task for the early years professional. It requires a very good understanding of current policies and practices, such as EYFS. In your search for pedagogy in the early years, it is important to look at other pedagogical practices to further your understanding. In studying other effective practices, you should not seek to transfer them to your own practice without adaptation, but adopt a critical approach in order to compare and reflect on your own practice, and also to enrich your understanding of early years pedagogy.

While this chapter aimed to discuss issues around different views that influence pedagogy, we will return to the discussion of pedagogy and curriculum in chapter 8, after building a theoretical and practical understanding of observation as a tool for practice and as a tool for research.

SUMMARY

This chapter aimed to discuss the influential constructions of childhood and philosophical approaches and developmental theories in early years, in an attempt to search for some principles for forming a pedagogy. The chapter presented a main emphasis on the ideas of Piaget and Vygotsky, and how these apply to an early years class. In the search for a pedagogical framework, some conditions of learning were identified:

- *emphasis on children's development;*
- *emphasis on children's play;*
- *emphasis on children's needs;*
- *emphasis on children's freedom to choose materials and activities;*
- *emphasis on children's ownership of their learning.*

The following chapter will discuss observations in this context.

For more on different approaches to pedagogy:

Clark, A, Kjorholt, AT and Moss, P (eds.) (2005) *Beyond Listening: children's perspectives on early childhood services.* Bristol: Policy Press.

Leach, J and Moon, B (2008) *The Power of pedagogy.* London: SAGE.

Taguchi, HL (2010) *Going beyond the theory/practice divide in early childhood education: Introducing intra-active pedagogy.* London: Routledge.

For more on constructions on childhood:

James, A and Prout, A (1997) *Constructing and reconstructing childhood* (2nd ed.). London: Falmer.

Kellet, M (2010) *Rethinking Children and Research: Attitudes in Contemporary Society.* London: Continuum.

For more on key influential thinkers in early childhood education:

Miller, L and Pound, L (eds.) (2010) *Theories and approaches to learning in the early years.* London: SAGE.

For more on philosophers and thinkers in education:

Palmer, JA (ed.) (2001) *Fifty Modern Thinkers in Education: From Piaget to the Present.* London: Routledge.

2 The role of observation in early years

Through reading this chapter, you will:

- understand the nature of observation within early childhood education and care and how this is related to early years practice;

- relate observations within current policy and evaluate the extent to which this affects your practice;

- identify and reflect on connections between knowledge and understanding of early childhood education and on the role of systematic observation within this context.

Observation is central to early childhood education as it provides a systematic way of understanding children's development and learning and responding to children's interests.

Introduction: Observation in context

Throughout this book the role of observation in early childhood education and its importance will be explored. Discussed in more detail in Chapter 8, observations play an important role in early childhood curriculum and practice. One of the main principles outlined within the EYFS (2008) clearly states that observations, assessment and planning are all central elements of practice within the early years setting. It emphasises that these observations of children should prioritise a child's development and learning. At the same time it stresses the importance of observations in terms of planning activities. The role of observation in early childhood education is a subject of ongoing discussion as the basis for planning practice that enhances children's development and learning.

For example, in 1990 the Rumbold Report emphasised the importance of assessment in context:

> We believe there is a need for guidance for educators on the achievement of more consistent and coherent approaches to observing, assessing, recording and reporting children's progress in preschools provision [. . .] such guidance is to inform and to improve on what is offered to the under fives and the early stages of the post five provision.
>
> (DfES, Rumbold Report, 1990, page 17)

Ten years later, one of the key principles identified within the Curriculum Guidance for the Foundation Stage was that *practitioners must be able to observe and respond appropriately to children, informed by a knowledge of how children develop and learn* (QCA, 2000, page 11).

Today there are expectations for the early years workforce to be able to observe, record and assess young children. The Early Years Foundation Stage (DfE, 2012a), implemented in September 2008 and revised in March 2012 (DfE, 2012a), had four main principles:

- an emphasis on the individual child as a learner (unique child);

- a recognition of the interpersonal relationships and the loving environment that all children need in order to develop (positive relationships);

- an appreciation of the learning environment as a vehicle for all children's development and learning (enabling environments);

- an identification of children's individual ways of personal development (learning and development).

As a statutory document, these principles aimed to inform the work of all early years workforce. The early years workforce has now changed since the introduction of the Early Years Professional Status (EYPS) in 2007. Currently there are over 8,300 EYPs working across England and there are about 1,800 learners who continue to undertake training to gain their full EYPS qualification (CWDC, 2012 n.p.)

Although when this book is written the EYPS standards are under review, according to the standards introduced in 2006, two of the standards that EYP candidates must be able to meet within their own practice (and also lead and support others) in order to achieve Early Years Professional Status, relate directly to observing children to:

- *assess, record, and report on progress in children's development and learning, and use this as a basis for differentiating provision* (CWDC, 2006, S21, page 7)

- *use close, informed observation and other strategies to monitor children's activity, development and progress systematically and carefully, and to use this information to inform, plan and improve upon practice and provision* (S10).

In addition, the Tickell review (2011) suggested an *improved* EYFS and recommended strongly a re-examination of the content of early years training courses alongside the quality of the qualifications, a view that was strongly supported in Professor Cathy Nutbrown's interim report on early education and childcare qualifications, published in March 2012. It is now more important than ever that a graduate early years workforce is promoted, and that its professional development is supported by encouraging those who are employed in the sector to gain further qualifications and thus improve the quality of provision.

Consequently, an early years workforce needs to be aware of the relevance of systematic methods of observation, for gathering evidence of children's behaviour and their interactions with their environment.

Observations have traditionally been used in the early years sector to influence practice. For example, Montessori (1912) introduced the Montessori Method, a systematic, scientific way of observing children in order to develop an early years practice based on their needs and focusing on physical needs, especially movement and play. She designed child-friendly material such as small chairs, tables, activities to help children develop their senses, literacy skills and numeracy strategies. Issacs (1933) brought psychoanalytical ideas of observation to the educational setting to develop a pedagogy for children that was connected with emotional development and encouraged play as a way by which children could express, discover and master the world.

Despite the importance of the role of observation that was emphasised in the early years sector, observations were formalised in 2008 by EYFS as a tool to assess children's progress and inform planning. The statutory requirements for teaching and assessing young children in the Early Years Foundation Stage (DCSF, 2008a) mean that it is essential to develop a more systematic approach to observations.

ACTIVITY **1**

How are observations used in the early years setting you are currently working in?

The early years workforce is moving towards that of a multi-disciplinary and multi-professional one. That means that professionals from different sectors (such as Education, Social Work, Psychology and Health) will work together in order to meet the *Every Child Matters* five outcomes:

- be healthy;

- be safe;

- enjoy and achieve;

- make a positive contribution;

- achieve economic well-being.

Outlined within *Every Child Matters* is the Common Assessment Framework (CAF) for children and young people. The CAF aims to be used with children who are at risk of failing to meet the five Every Child Matters outcomes (HM Government, 2006b). The Common Assessment Framework (HM Government, 2006b) has been introduced, and it is a requirement that all professionals should be able to communicate and share information effectively about children. It states that *it is particularly suitable for use in universal services (health, education, etc), to identify and tackle problems before they become serious.*

The Common Assessment Framework is designed to become a preventative tool in the hands of the early years professional. Throughout the CAF there is an emphasis on the *common assessment processes* by all key staff working with children, in order to meet their needs. It also recognises that the CAF aims to formalise existing practices in many sectors, but also to become the basis for creating a portrait for children, where needs are met and satisfied and where early interventions are taking place in a pro-active manner. A fully implemented Common Assessment Framework includes the collection of information on a child's development. Parents/carers and the family environment are involved in this process. The areas covered in a common assessment are:

- development of the infant child and young person;

- health;

- development (physical development, speech, language and communication development, emotional and social development, behavioural development, identity – including self-esteem, self-image, and social presentation);

- family and social relationships;

- self-care skills and independence;

- learning (understanding, reasoning and problem solving, participation in learning, education and employment, progress and achievement in learning, and aspirations);

- safety and protection;

- emotional warmth and stability.

ACTIVITY 2

Read the Common Assessment Framework for children and young people: Practitioners Guide (Sections 5 and 6). You can access this document from the following web page:

www.cwdcouncil.org.uk/assets/0000/9081/CAF_Practitioner_Guide.pdf

Reflect on the areas that are covered in a common assessment. Do they offer a good and helpful basis for your work with babies and young children?

In this context, this chapter discusses the nature of observations. It begins by looking at why early years practitioners carry out observations. It considers the skills that practitioners should develop as one of the main factors involved when working with young children.

The nature of observations

Although there is a wealth of literature about observations, Drummond (1998) suggests that we ought to develop manageable systems for being able to watch children interacting with one another and their environment, in order to create comprehensive portraits of children as autonomous individuals.

> *[. . .] Observing learning, [and] getting close to children's minds and children's feelings, is part of our daily work in striving for quality [. . .] Our careful observations of children's learning can help us make [early years] provision better. We can use what we see to identify the strengths and weaknesses, gaps and inconsistencies, in what we provide. We can identify significant moments in a child's learning, and we can build on what we see.*
> (Drummond, 1998, page 105)

When considering the nature of observations, the main goal should be to help practitioners understand child development and learning and to help them plan their activities and practices, based on children's needs as learners; it should also help to create an environment where this will *play a key role in supporting and extending children's development and learning* (EYFS, 2012b, page 3). However, carrying out observations requires skills and expertise as Nutbrown and Carter emphasise: *Watching children as they learn and understanding their learning moments is complex and difficult work and places the highest of demands upon their educators* (2010, page 120).

On the basis of this, when the nature of observations is discussed, it is important to understand the term comprehensively. Gillham (2008, page 1) claims that observation *deals not with what people say they do but what they* actually *do*. Observation is a systematic method of studying human behaviour or phenomena within a specific context and should always have a precise purpose. It involves key cognitive dimensions: attention, working memory, perception and time, as it requires recording and watching over a period of time. Smith (1998, page 6) claims that observation is a *deliberate, active process, carried out with care and forethought, of noting events as they occur.* As will be mentioned later in this chapter, observation is a complex activity, because the way we *see* (perception) other people and their behaviours is related to our self-experiences as we all have a *preferred way of viewing ourselves* (Gillham, 2008, page 1) and others. Our skills, such as focusing intensively for a period of time (attention) and working memory capacity, are also unique to the individual. All these factors make observation a highly skilled method.

Observations as a systematic method of using particular ways to look at and record children's behaviours should always have a clear intention. In an attempt to define observations in the early years context, we might argue that it is a valid tool for understanding children's development, in order to help early years practitioners to assess their development. The term 'observe' literally means 'to look at', to 'watch something closely'. The term 'observation' is used to describe the systematic and *structured way* (Faragher and MacNaughton, 1998) in which the early years workforce views children in order to understand them, with the ultimate purpose of assessing their development and inform any future planning. This systematic way of scrutinising children enables us to help to understand in depth children's development, gain insight into children's daily routines and therefore be a useful resource, not only in training of early years practitioners, but also as a way of deepening early years practice.

At another level, by observing what children do, we understand their development, and the way in which they behave and react within certain situations and contexts. This reflection informs not only our early years practice, but is also an important channel of communication for the children's families.

ACTIVITY 3

With reference to Early Years Foundation Stage try to answer the following questions:
1. *What place do observations have in your setting?*
2. *How do they inform your practice?*
3. *How could you use observations to help you learn more about children?*
   If possible, try to pose the same questions to a more experienced early years practitioner in your setting and then compare your answers.

Observations for a reason

Observations are the *foundation of education in the early years* (Hurst, 1991, page 70). The main reason that observations are part of early years practice, and are subsequently emphasised by the EYFS, is that they can offer us important information about children, their abilities and their interests, that are not available elsewhere. Furthermore, closely watching children via systematic techniques – as will be described in the following chapter – can give the observers and the early years professional an in-depth look at children. This can enhance our understanding of children and their actions. Observations focus on a child's natural behaviour in a given setting, which is the key process for assessing their development. Looking at children closely helps observers to recognise stages of child development, and to take responsibility for helping a child to progress.

Through the systematic collection of information about children, professionals are able to gather a number of incidents and evidence, which can then offer an accurate picture about children's behaviours and development. This evidence, gathered through observations, is a very important tool in the hands of professionals, especially in the case of dealing with very young children. Young children have a limited repertoire of language and behaviours – and when professionals are asked to explain and to try to provide a supportive learning environment for young children, it is necessary to be able to understand the children involved first and foremost. Young children, through their play and through their interaction with others, make meaningful suggestions about their thoughts and feelings. Thus, via observations, professionals can collect accurate and pertinent data about these children. Accordingly, the most accurate way for professionals to study children is through these observations.

Systematic observations also help professionals to understand the reasons behind children's behaviour in certain situations. Benjamin (1994) emphasises their importance: *Observations play an important role in assessment, either by replacing or by supplementing standardised evaluation instruments* (Benjamin, 1994, page 14).

Consequently, observers can recognise stages of child development, relate these to the theoretical stages of normal development, and then subsequently take responsibility for helping a child's progress. In this sense, observations not only help the early years professionals' practice, but also provide a reliable context for them to make links between theory and practice, in order to demonstrate what they have learned about children.

Observations allow theory to be exercised in a practical context and allow professionals the opportunity to implement theory in their daily practice. It is by no means presumptuous to say that observations facilitate professionals' reflective thinking and thus empower them to evaluate their own practice in an attempt to develop effectively. Thus there is a dual purpose to observations: first and foremost, to help professionals understand children, but also to help professionals to progress within their own practice through reflection.

Observations focus on what a child *can* do (and not on what a child *cannot* do) as a basis for forward planning. It is important to highlight what a child is capable of, in order to plan activities. An observation's main focus is on what children can achieve. Moreover, it is in the nature of observations to focus on a child's natural behaviour within the early years setting. The information collected can be a valid starting point for assessing a child and his or her development.

Observations offer an in-depth look at a child not available in other ways. Discussion with the parents can offer an insight about their children within the family environment, which is a very helpful tool for professionals. However, there is a necessity for early years workers to try and investigate children's behaviour within the context of the classroom.

A body of contemporary literature (Clark and Moss, 2001; Clark *et al.*, 2005; Rinaldi, 2006) are promoting observation as a way of listening to children and giving voices to them. Luff (2007) stresses *observing and documenting learning can be a way of valuing and listening to children* (page 189). Elfer (2005) adds that within current legislation, such as the requirements raised by the Children's Act (HMSO, 2004) and the United Nations Convention on Children's Rights (1989), observations can provide an effective context for listening to children's attempts to communicate and for professionals to take into consideration a child's distinctive voice.

Thus observations can become a suitable path for opening up communication with children. Evidence through observations helps professionals to consider children's voices and their needs and experiences, in order to create pedagogical activities that will comply with children's interests. This can create learning environments for children that are not only safe, enjoyable and applicable, but also exciting. However, one should be very careful about how to use observations as a way of listening to children or offering voices to children as, in an attempt to observe in early years settings, there are occasions where the privacy of children's conversations with other children is violated. There are questions about to what extent as early years practitioners we have the right to photograph and record children's activities and where we draw the line where something is private among children. All these ethical concerns will be discussed in Chapter 5.

It is in the nature of observations to provide opportunities for collaboration. The multi-professional workforce should seek ways of communicating and sharing information and ideas about their understanding of children, in order to *promote earlier interventions . . . [and to] improve quality* (HM Government, 2006b). The basis of multi-disciplinary work can be provided by evidence collected via observations to *embed a common language about the needs of children* (HM Government, 2006b).

ACTIVITY 4

1. *Consider your Early Years setting and try to think of any occasions where observations became a suitable source for listening to children and what action you subsequently took.*

2. *Can you recall any opportunities where you used information from observations to work in a multi-professional way?*

Here we will argue that observations should be viewed as part of the daily routine of the classroom and not as a separate tool that professionals can use as and when they need it. Observation is *not* a tool where children with a problem are studied in an attempt to resolve dilemmas. These are instances when there is a specific problem with a child. Observations ought to be implemented as part of *everyday* practice. Observations, as a purposeful tool, should focus on children's development and learning, and an interpretation of observations as a reflection on daily practice which *is unobtrusively woven into classroom activity and interaction* (Pratt, 1994, page 102).

Te Whaariki and observations

An example of how observations have been integrated or 'woven' into the everyday life of the classroom comes from New Zealand. As discussed in Chapter 1, the curriculum of New Zealand aims to create a multicultural learning environment. Te Whaariki is underpinned by five goals:

- well-being;

- belonging;

- contribution;

- communication;

- exploration.

Consequently, observations look at the behaviours that are central to children. These behaviours are important for the development of children as effective learners. Carr (2001) stresses the importance of children obtaining these behaviours, and suggests the following model of assessment and observation:

The strands of the curriculum	The behaviour we look at
Belonging	Taking an interest
Well-being	Being involved
Exploration	Persisting with difficulty, challenges and uncertainty
Communication	Expressing a point of view or feeling
Contribution	Taking responsibility

In Carr's work, as mentioned above, observation is central to the curriculum. It is integrated in the daily practice of the class – *woven within the curriculum*. It is important to see that observation has a definite purpose and that this purpose is oriented by curriculum learning objectives and outcomes.

Carr claims that observations are central in creating *learning communities [. . .] where children [can]*:

- *take an interest in an activity;*

- *become involved in it over a sustained period of time;*

- *persist when they meet difficulty, challenges or uncertainty;*

- *express their ideas or feelings in a range of ways;*

- *take responsibility to change the way things are, to teach others and to listen to another point of view.*

(Carr, 1998, page 15)

According to Carr, these processes are linear and they appear in sequence; thus she characterises them as *Learning Stories*. The main interest/focus of these learning stories is the merging of dispositions and the accompanying people, places and phenomena that make the emergence more likely and how early years practitioners can strengthen these dispositions. The importance of these learning stories is that they provide guidelines for the adults' planning of activities and which, in addition, can also provide families with an insight into their children's day, giving the parents a view of learning that is valued and encouraged.

So we can see, in the curriculum the use of observation is two-fold: firstly, to help and improve early years practitioners' practice, pedagogy and activities; and, secondly, as a valid tool to communicate with the children's families. In addition, the children themselves participate in writing these stories. Therefore observations in the Te Whaariki classroom are part of daily life and routine and they are used not only in certain circumstances, but as part of the curriculum as a whole, in order to be able to monitor a child's progress.

ACTIVITY 5

Carry out an audit of these types of observations that are carried out daily in your setting.

How can these observations be integrated within the implementation of EYFS?

Why observe children?

As noted above, observations formalise the link between theory and practice, so professionals are able to demonstrate what they have learned about children across all areas.

THEORY FOCUS

- There is a need for a systematic way of making observations within the learning environment.

- Observations are the structured way of studying children.

- Observations inform pedagogy and curriculum structure.

- Observations underpin the everyday activities of the classroom.

- Observations can become the tool for multi-professional collaboration.

Observations help us to:

- collect and gather evidence that can offer an accurate picture of children, their learning and development;

- understand the reasons behind children's behaviour in certain situations;

- recognise stages in child development;

- inform planning and assessment;

- provide opportunities for collaboration with parents and other services;

- find out about children as individuals;

- monitor progress;

- inform curriculum planning;

- enable staff to evaluate their practice;

- provide a focus for discussion and improvement.

Thus far we have discussed what observations should look at. In this section we will briefly discuss what observations should aim towards. To begin with, observations as a methodological tool, in the hands of an early years professional, address a child's development. All aspects of development are under scrutiny where children are involved. Emotional, social, physical, cognitive and moral awareness are all crucial aspects of a child's progress and these are all interlinked. We might, as early years professionals, study and observe them separately, but they all come together in order to offer us a complete portrait of an individual child's development and progress.

All children go through observable sequences of behaviour at their own pace, and this sequence of development can be traced by the early years professional from the perspective of an observer. The main issue is that the early years professional should know what to look and listen for in each instance.

CASE STUDY

Read the following case study and try to:
 identify which areas of development Sue needs encouragement in;

- use The Development Matters in EYFS pages 8–14 (DfE, 2012b) as your guideline in order to complete the activity;

- consider how you can help Sue and her parents.

Sue's story:

Sue is a two-year-old girl. She is the only child in her family. She has joined the early years setting three weeks ago. She is a lively and active child, but she cries a lot every day and the early years practitioners cannot calm her. She appears to be in distress, sad and stressed when her mother leaves her in the morning. She does not interact with other children and she only wants to be in the company of the adults. She does not want to share any toys when she plays, and during the activities she sits quietly and does not talk to other children. She appears not to interact with other children and has not made any friends.

Becoming a skilful observer

As has been demonstrated previously, observations are a purposeful and a daily reflective tool for gathering information about children's behaviour, their needs and their development, and this task requires a skilful professional. This section aims to offer guidance on how to become a skilful observer discussing factors involved when we prepare observations.

Observation aims and objectives

As observation is a systematic method to collect evidence of children's behaviour, it is important to set clear aims and objectives. There is a need to distinguish what is meant by aims and objectives.

Aims are about what you intend to observe and what you want to achieve. They are therefore focused, precise and unambiguous. For example, they are on an area of development such as physical or social development, or on an activity that has been introduced in the setting to encourage children's language interactions, such as telephone area. Objectives are about specific skills or abilities you want to observe; thus they are detailed reasons for observation, achievable, measurable and realistic, linked with children's development and your practice. In that sense objectives are considered as the steps by which you achieve your aims.

You work in the baby room and you want to observe the babies' emotional development. Here is an example of possible aims and objectives when you observe emotional development. Try to develop your own objectives for distress, affection, enjoyment and interest in activities.

Aim: Emotional development	Objectives
Shows interest in materials	*When exploring materials, possible observed objectives:* Directing eyes towards materials Touching materials Exploring materials for a period of time Showing intensity Showing apathy Showing a lot/little movement Touching materials with care Kicking materials Throwing materials Dropping materials Showing curiosity
How fear is expressed	*When experiencing unfamiliar faces possible observed objectives:* Crying Whining Clinging Hiding behind objects Tightening muscles Closing eyes sharply for a period of time Shouting Trembling Runs/crawls away Puts hands on face (hiding with his/her hands) Seeks one of the practitioners
How anger is expressed	*When baby is physically or psychological frustrated possible observed objective:* Feeling disappointed when child cannot achieve something Feeling irritated when child cannot achieve something Frowning when child cannot achieve Shouting Red face Loud words Aggression Biting Beating Crying Withdrawing Screaming

Table 2.1   Aims and objectives when observing emotional development

As mentioned earlier in this chapter, when the early years team is planning how individual children's profiles will be built and when developing strategies of evaluating the educational programme and its activities, observations are the tool for collecting this evidence. It is important that members of the early years team share roles and responsibilities before they start, and clarify and set aims and objectives for the observations. This way the team will remain focused and collect rich evidence to effectively complete each child's profile, and to evaluate the educational programme itself.

Aims and objectives for undertaking the observations should be clearly defined, as the objectives will determine the nature of the information to be gathered.

Working within the EYFS, the learning and development goals need to be met, but due to the broad nature of the learning areas it is important to set clear objectives. These will enable the gathering of comprehensive evidence around each goal. Clear aims and objectives will also allow you to choose the most appropriate observation technique. As inclusive practitioners, aims and objectives ought to be shared with parents and the carers of children and be modified in the light of subsequent comments.

Observation planning should involve the whole team in the process of agreeing who will carry out the observations and ensure that all team members gain the valuable experience of undertaking observations.

Clear roles within the classroom setting should be decided, so that the practitioner undertaking the observation knows when to remove him or herself from activities in preparation to observe. It is also important that children know in advance who is the observer in that activity – although, of course with very young children this cannot always be achieved.

Objectivity

One of the key skills that early years professionals should develop is objectivity. This is always a main aspiration. It is a challenging aspect of the observation and takes much practice, thus ensuring as far as possible that, as professionals, we are as objective as possible and so record what *actually* happens, and not what we merely *assume* to be happening. However, the issue of achieving objectivity is a difficult one and can mislead the early years workforce. As mentioned above the aim of observation is to record in a systematic way what we actually do. In that sense one might claim that this is objectivity. However, we cannot ignore that how we represent the world or events is related to our perception which in turn is influenced by our own experiences, emotions, self-image and self-perception or of what 'reality' is. In such contexts, objectivity is relative. One should seek for subjective 'reality' (Gillham, 2008) and try to collect as much evidence as possible, using a plethora of collection techniques in order to avoid the trap of seeing what we *want* to see or *assume* to have seen, rather than the reality of events. A video recording of the same scenario may well differ from our notes of it, despite the intended honesty of the observer.

The following activity attempts to demonstrate how difficult it is to be objective and to record what actually does take place.

ACTIVITY 7

Look at the picture and write down what you see. Then show the picture to a colleague or to a fellow student or EYP candidate, and ask this person to do the same. Now compare your answers. Are they the same? Do you see what it is actually there?

Figure 2.1 Children at the book area

Have you written, 'There are two boys reading books'?

But what do you actually see? *You see two boys holding books. Whether these two boys read the books is an interpretation of what is seen. What we can actually observe is the following: two boys are holding and looking at books.*

This is a clear example of one of the main challenges when we observe young children. It is difficult to step out of our personal values, beliefs and cultural stereotypes, and to retain objectivity when we record our observations.

Consequently, the second challenge for the professional is not only to step back from personal values, beliefs and culture, but also to step out of the role that these normally signify. There are times when the systematic observer should not interfere with the activity of the child in question. Within the daily life of the classroom, the early years professional is faced with a number of tasks, and when he or she has to deliver activities with the children it is challenging to step out of the 'educator' role and become an observer. This is a constant exercise and it will be discussed more comprehensively in the next chapter.

It is important that when an observation is taking place the observer judges to what extent the collection of information is 'disturbed'. In such a case the observer needs to stop the observation if the child or children, is/are distracted or the observation is unduly distorted, as attention and concentration on the task will be lost.

The challenging task of observation not only requires objectivity – in addition to training to distance yourself from your normal role as a systematic observer – but also to consider that your emotions are involved. As Willan argues:

> Both child and observer come with their own load of emotional baggage. The child being observed or assessed has feelings, as do the parents, carers and educators around him/her – and so, of course, does the observer. It is important to be aware of the emotional dimension of the observational context, and to try to take it into account as part of the assessment process.
>
> (2007, page 109)

The process of observation takes place in the natural environment of the child and the early years setting where children stay for a great amount of their day. Within this context there are a number of pressures for the early years professional. There is always the pressure for children to be safe, for them to be able to participate and enjoy activities, and there is also the additional pressure of being capable of observing objectively without bringing any values, beliefs or stereotypes into the process.

In this context observers should assume an emotionally unbiased attitude towards the subject. However, it is often difficult to achieve such an emotionally unbiased equilibrium.

Luff adds to this point and elaborates upon another difficulty:

> The processes for learning using documentation are, therefore, highly complex. An additional challenge for English early years professionals is a requirement to work in two potentially contradictory ways. On the one hand, observations can create opportunities to plan according to carefully looking at, and listening to, children's actions and responses; on the other hand, early years professionals are expected to work towards specific pre-set learning outcomes. As skilled professionals, early years practitioners must therefore gain confidence in demonstrating how specified criteria can be met through flexible holistic ways of working, [and] also need to find means of using structured guidelines, such as the EYFS, as frameworks for their observations.
>
> (2007, page 187)

Team involvement

As mentioned above, it is essential for the whole team to be involved in the observation process. The team needs to share ownership of this and be clear that all of them work on common aims and objectives. One of the main limitations of observation is that what is observed needs to be recorded – and practitioners will return to this after either a long day of work or after a certain period of time. When the events are subsequently read and analysed, the factors that lead a child to behave in a certain way, or which led to the success or otherwise of an activity, might have been forgotten and the record of the events loses its meaning. Important information might be missing or cannot be remembered. If possible, not only events should be recorded but the possible reasons for these, so that future reviews of the notes, possibly by other professionals that were not involved in the process at the time, are meaningful. In this way valid conclusions can be drawn from the event. Team involvement is important as objectivity is very difficult to achieve. Each of us has our own values and system of beliefs; we are part of a social or cultural group and this influences the way we observe. A plethora of observations (the same ones from different people) will offer a pluralistic portrait of what actually happens in children's development and learning. Such an approach will lead to a closer 'accurate' interpretation of the observation findings.

Team involvement in the observation process can also work as a way of mentoring less experienced early years practitioners and guiding them in the process through peer interaction. Moreover, each member of the team can bring different expertise and experiences so that putting them together will enrich the observation planning and broaden its scope. Observation planning can also work as a team-building process. During team meetings and involvement there are often opportunities to develop a culture of critical ear and analysis of policy, diverse perspectives, and create positive interactions with all members of the team. Team involvement in observation planning can become a valid opportunity to communicate information, in order to try to solve problems before they arise. Finally and equally importantly, through ownership of the observation planning by all members of the team, an ethos of mutual trust is built. Members of the team will not feel intimidated, threatened or 'afraid' when observations are taking place as they share ownership of the process.

Parental involvement

In addition to these skills, there is also a need to involve parents in the observation of their children. As mentioned earlier, observations can become a valid path of communication between early years professionals and the children's families. Parental involvement is important in the assessment of their children. Involving the parents encourages them to feel that they are participating in the life of their children whilst they are in the early years setting. Moreover, parents feel more comfortable about their child's daily life in the classroom, and this subsequently minimises the risk of feeling inordinately judged by the early years environment. The involvement of parents in the observation planning helps break down barriers between professionals and the parents. Asking for parents' help might assist early years professionals to achieve emotionally unbiased skills, and to offer a more in-depth insight into other aspects of the children's behaviour and subsequently into the development that is under scrutiny.

Child involvement

As well as involving the parents, it is essential the children can also be heard within this process as participants (see Chapter 3). Observations in the daily classroom environment offer opportunities for listening to children's own voices. Clark and Moss (2001) carried out a study aiming to search *for a way to listen to young children [talk] about their lives* (page 11), and demonstrate the effects of listening to children and suggested ways of doing this.

As a result, they developed the Mosaic approach, a way of not only listening to children's distinct voices (a requirement of the EYFS, Children's Act and the United Nations Convention on Children's Rights, as mentioned earlier), but also as a way of ensuring children's views are respected in an empowering way for the child. Clark and Moss (2001) describe fundamental conditions for empowering children's voices, when we create such an environment.

Firstly, they introduce a *climate of listening* whereby children's experiences, interests and views influence their relationships to adults and to their environment.

Secondly, they stress the importance of allowing time to listen to children. The Mosaic approach involves a time of communication for early years staff in several ways:

- gathering the material will take longer because we are not relying on a single method of communication;

- interpreting the material gathered is time consuming (page 64).

Thirdly, they also emphasise the significant place of staff training, not only in order to listen to children, but also training in terms of understanding children's development – and the ways in which children make attempts to communicate and learn the skills that they will use throughout their lives.

THEORY FOCUS

Read the following extract and try to identify the main skills that early years professionals should develop in order to become competent observers.

Which of these skills do you feel you already have?

One of the greatest challenges is the need to be objective and unbiased. We must not allow objectivity to be influenced by pre-conceived ideas about the child's attainment.

Observation can also be a time-consuming process. It does need to be carefully organized and managed within the setting or classroom, so that everyone is aware of their role and responsibility, in relation to observation and assessment. It is essential to involve all those working with children in the observation and assessment process, and this needs careful organization, management and training for all those who are going to be carrying out these processes. Devising ways of integrating observation into practice within a reception class, particularly if there are no additional adults working with you, requires creativity and a commitment to the value of this as an essential tool for your professional practice. Observation can also be professionally demanding for practitioners. These demands can take the form of being surprised or threatened by the information gathered through observation. When gathering observation data it is also likely that one will be observing the adults working with children more carefully than usual, and this may also engender a sense of fear and anxiety within the adults. A final challenge to practitioners is that of interpreting or analyzing the information that has been gathered. You need to use your

THEORY FOCUS *continued*

understanding of child development, along with your professional knowledge, to interpret what you see and hear and take the child's learning forward or change your own practice. This is often best achieved through discussions with all those involved in the setting, including nursery nurses, teaching assistants, key workers and other practitioners. A key factor in this process of interpretation is ensuring that the evidence you are working with is gathered objectively, and accurately, taking account of the challenges that are identified above.

Hamilton, C, Haywood, S, Gibbins, S, McInnes, K and Williams, J (2003) *Principles and Practice in the Foundation Stage.* Learning Matters (page 61).

Observation planning

As mentioned in the previous section, the process of becoming a skilful observer is complex and challenging. It requires constant self-development, self-assessment, an addressing of individual needs and the overcoming of personal emotional boundaries. Thus it is important to invest time and effort in observation planning, before embarking on it. During the planning stage, the aims and objectives should be described clearly so all involved in the process (children, parents, team members) know what they are doing and feel confident about this. Team, parental and child involvement are essential in your observational planning. Good observation planning should consider the following questions:

- What steps (objectives) do we need to take in order to reach our aim/aims?
- How can we gain more information in relation to a particular child or children?
- How can we gain more information in relation to the implementation of the curriculum?
- How can we involve the children?
- How can we involve the team so all of them feel comfortable and confident?
- How can we involve parents?

The next step is to choose your observation techniques and develop them to fit to your own context (it will be explored in Chapter 3). Finally the last step is to decide which ways you will employ to record and document your observations and findings (see Chapter 4).

SUMMARY

This chapter has investigated the nature of observations within the contemporary early years setting. In the light of the current Government policies, these observations hold an important and essential role. The early years workforce is asked more than ever to use observations as a systematic way of assessing children within EYFS.

Observation is a valid tool to understand children's development and learning and inform practice. It has a key role in early years practice as it helps us to find out about children, monitor their progress, inform curriculum planning, enable staff to evaluate the

SUMMARY *continued*

provisions they make, provide a focus for discussion and improvement and understand early years practice better. It has been emphasised throughout this chapter that observations should be 'woven' into early years daily practice and not seen as an external aspect of our work.

In that sense, it is important that all early years practitioners have training in order to become skilful observers. In the daily routine of early years practice and as a systematic observer of children, you will need to develop objectivity and an absence of emotional bias, and you must therefore first step out of the role that you normally hold. As highlighted in Chapter 5, part of the observation planning is the ethical considerations of the planning and this should be based on team, parental and child involvement – and confidentiality is an essential element in the whole process. Before we explore this, it is important to study the observation techniques. The next chapter attempts to discuss the variety of observation techniques that are available to the professional.

FURTHER
READING

For more general information on observation in early childhood education:

Papatheodorou, T, Luff, P and Gill, J (2011) *Child Observation for Learning and Research.* Essex: Pearson Education.

Podmore, VN and Luff, P (2011) *Observation.* Maidenhead: Open University Press.

For more information on how observation is used for assessment purposes:

Carr, M (2001) *Assessment in Early Childhood Settings.* London: SAGE.

Drummond, MJ (2003) *Assessing Children's Learning* (2nd ed.) London: David Fulton.

Drummond, MJ (1998) *Observing Children*, in Smidt, S (ed.) *The Early Years: A Reader.* London: Routledge.

For more on the Mosaic approach and children's participation:

Clark, A and Moss, P (2006) *Listening to children: The Mosaic approach.* London: National Children's Bureau and Joseph Rowntree Foundation.

WEBSITES

For government documents:

EYFS www.foundationyears.org.uk

CAF for EYPS information www.education.gov.uk/publications

3   Observation techniques

Through reading this chapter, you should understand:

- the most common observation techniques;

- how observations can help you to collect information for each child's assessment;

- how observation techniques can help you collect information for evaluation of the educational programme.

There are a number of observation techniques available to early years practitioners and professionals depending on the purposes of the observation.

Introduction

The Statutory Framework for the EYFS asserts that:

> ongoing assessment (also known as formative assessment) is an integral part of the learning and development process. It involves practitioners observing children to understand their level of achievement, interests and learning styles, and then shape learning experiences for each child reflecting on those observations.
>
> (DfE, 2012a, page 10)

It is also stated that all the evidence for children's assessment should have been gathered by observational recordings. Within this requirement there is a necessity for the early years professional to be aware of the variety of observation techniques. This chapter aims to explore these techniques which are there are to help the professionals involved with children.

As explained in Chapter 2, observations should always have a purpose. For the early years professional working with EYFS this purpose is clearly stated. The general and ultimate goal of observations is to collect information to give as complete a picture as possible of the child for assessment purposes. However, in this chapter, it will be stressed that observations can have the important secondary aim of collecting information to enable practitioners to evaluate their own educational programmes, activities and curriculum, and through this systematic evidence, inform future planning. Throughout this chapter, these observational techniques will be explored. It is important to emphasise that each technique has its place and role in the early years sector and, in order to have an effective complete picture of children's learning and development, the early years workforce should master and employ a number of techniques.

Observation methods

There are three types of observation that have been developed from the field of social research and which can be used in early years settings' day-to-day practice. These are: unstructured observations (participant), structured observations (non-participant) and semi-structured observations. The theory focus box and paragraphs that follow describe these methods and their techniques, as well as offering an evaluation of them.

Three types of observation: advantages and disadvantages

Methods	Description	Purpose	Advantages	Disadvantages
Unstructured observation (Participant observation)	The observer is part of the normal daily life of the group being observed. Normally the observer belongs to the group (for example is an early years practitioner). It is naturalistic observation in the sense that events are observed as they occur.	It aims to capture what children do in that setting on a particular day, as they participate in the activity. Notes are kept to be checked afterwards with other team members. The aim is to collect evidence which will support the description of an activity event or behaviour. Other materials may be used such as photographs, videos, drawings or other relevant documents to support the description of the event.	Provides useful insight into activities, behaviours. It is not time consuming as it happens as the events occur. Requires minimum preparation. Captures unexpected behaviours or changes in an activity.	It is difficult to interpret if not supported by other evidence as it relies on memory. It might be based on the perspective of the observer only (lack of objectivity). It can be very detailed and descriptive and it might distract from its significance. It is time consuming. Information collected can be large and messy and requires too much organisation.
Semi-structured observation	The observation has clear aims and objectives but the methods are 'open' so unpredicted events can be captured.	It aims to capture events that cannot be predicted. It aims to discover WHY certain events or behaviours occur.	Provides in-depth information about the context and circumstances of a behaviour, event or activities. Helps you identify problems, good practices, strengths and weaknesses that you might have not considered.	You might miss out events or behaviours you considered normal and to be expected. It is time-consuming as you need to spend time in the setting. It can be messy. It requires careful interpretation and cross-checking with other members of the team or other materials.

Structured observation (non-participant) (all the following techniques are part of the structured non-participant observations)	It is a clear focus observation on exact behaviours, events, activities.	It is mechanistic, as specific techniques are used, but it offers rigour through good information on an activity, event or behaviour.	Evidence collected is normally numerical and easy to be interpreted. Captures sequences of events, behaviours, activities. It does not require a lot of time (including the planning). Information collected can be easily organised and categorised.	Numerical information can be superficial and does not offer an in-depth approach to why certain events, behaviours occur.
Narratives: 1. Anecdotal records 2. Running records	Written description of an event, child's behaviour, activity. Anecdotal: brief narrative describing an event, behaviour, activity. Running: a sequence of written descriptions of a particular event, behaviour, activity.	They aim to record specific behaviours, events, activities and their progress over a period of time. Aim to discover why certain events, behaviours occur.	Offer rich information as the observer records everything that happens. The observer can capture significant, unexpected events, activities, behaviours.	They offer a complete picture of what has happened. They can be messy if not organised carefully. They rely on memory and attention of the individual so need to be cross-referenced with other materials, information. They are time-consuming. They require special training. Observer needs to remove him/herself from the children and this has an impact in the ratio of the classroom.
Sampling: 1. Time sampling 2. Event sampling	Captures samples of events, activities, behaviours. It is concerned with frequency (how often or rare) and duration.	It aims to observe certain behaviours over a period of time or over different activities.	It does not take much time. Children can participate as self-observers. Information can be collected for one child or a group of children at the same time with minimum effort from the observer. Offers useful information on intervals and frequencies.	It does not offer an explanation as to why an event or a behaviour has occurred. It needs to be used in conjunction with other methods. It is limited only to observable behaviours and other behaviours might be missed.

Rating scales: 1. Graphic scales 2. Numerical scales	A scale of events, behaviours recorded before, during or after the event.	It aims to rate the child's behaviour, involvement, participation in a certain activity, event.	Once designed, it does not take time from the observer. It is easy to design. You can observe more than one child at a time. It can be used by several observers for the same child. Children can participate in this method as self-observers.	It is limited only to the focus of the scale. You might miss other behaviours. Scale can be difficult to use if all observers have not understood the rating.
Checklists	They capture a list of behaviours or developmental steps.	They aim to identify whether or not a child or children has/have acquired certain behaviours or developmental characteristics.	Offer an overview of the development of a child or group of children. Once designed, they can be used again. They can be used by several observers. They can be used by children who can participate in self-observations.	They focus only on certain developmental characteristics or behaviours. They do not offer a rationale of why certain characteristics or behaviours occur. They need to be cross-referenced or supported by other methods.
Diagrammatic: 1. Histograms 2. Tracking 3. Sociograms 4. Bar charts and pie charts	This is a purpose-specific technique and captures a certain behaviour or aspect of development.	It aims to observe whether a certain behaviour or developmental aspect has or has not occurred.	It can be used by children as self-observers. Once designed, it can be used again for another group of children. Offers an overview of a behaviour or aspect of development.	It is limited to only one aspect of behaviour or development. It does not offer an explanation of why a behaviour is occurring. It needs to be cross-referenced with other methods.

Table 3.1   Three types of observation: advantages and disadvantages

Participant observation (unstructured)

As it is part of the daily routine, participant observation is well known within the early years profession. When early years professionals work with children they either record an event by writing down quick notes at the time of the event, or later after the event. These brief and immediate notes are part of an ongoing daily practice. The event is recorded when the professional is working with the children directly and he or she does not withdraw in order to observe. These recordings are usually brief comments about a child's behaviour during an activity, or are comments on how the activity was implemented.

There are a number of advantages when the professionals are using participant observation. The daily events recorded can provide the practitioner with a useful insight into a child or an activity. Special training is not required, as the professional writes down his/her perception of an event as it occurs. This type of observation is unstructured and observers write down what appears to them to be most interesting and relevant at the time. It does not require planning or organisation, and it is useful as events such as unexpected behaviour or an unexpected change within an activity are recorded.

However, there are obvious limitations to this method. Participant observation will not give a complete picture of the events and requires the professional to rely on memory, as events will be largely recorded after they have happened.

As Devereux (2003) points out, participant observation can be messy and difficult to manage. It should be categorised and filed immediately otherwise useful evidence could be lost. An additional disadvantage to this type of observation technique is that the recorded information could be examined long after an event, thus allowing the potential for an inaccurate and biased interpretation of events.

However, despite the disadvantages of using participant observation, it is a very simple and immediate tool to use in collecting information as events occur, and can be used to capture unexpected events during the day.

ACTIVITY 1

Can you list any further disadvantages of participant observation?

There are ways to help limit the disadvantages of this type of observation. Professionals can have pre-prepared forms to quickly record occurrences. The following information can be included:

> Name of the observer: _____
> Name of the child: _____
> Date of observation: _____
> Starting time: _____ Finishing time: _____
> No. of adults present: _____
> Area of observation: _____
> Description of the activity observed: _____
> Additional comments: _____
> I think _____ (In this section you add your thoughts that occurred during the observation, that they might help you later to interpret your recordings.)

Note: it might be helpful to create in-trays: one for activities, one for events and one with each child named in your setting where you put the observations recordings for activities, events, or named children. This way helps to categorise and organise observations and limit the messy factor of participant observation.

This obviously speeds up the recording process and facilitates the filing of recordings. Therefore, when the recordings are re-visited, all the information will be included, making retrieval and interpretation much easier.

Kenzie is four years and eleven months old. He has been absent from many of his classes. The aim of the observation is to identify whether or not these frequent absences are affecting his ability to make and sustain friendships.

Aim: to look for evidence of social play and participation.

Observation 1

Name of the observer: Emily (EYP)
Name of the child: Kenzie, 4 years and 11 months
Date of observation: 09/07/11
Starting time: 10:30
Finishing time: 10:34
No. of adults present: 1 adult
Area of observation: free play outdoors

Description of the activity observed:
It is an outdoor play time and Kenzie is in the corner of the playground kicking leaves that have fallen from a tree. He is on his own, smiling and his arms are waving freely as he kicks the leaves. Liam, who has been playing with a group of three other boys, approaches Kenzie and says 'Come and play. It's me, Jack and Tommy'. Kenzie drops his head, looking towards the floor and his arms and legs remain still whilst Liam is speaking to him. Liam returns to his group of friends without Kenzie, who continues to droop his head and remain motionless.

Additional comment:
Prior to Kenzie being approached by his peer, he was involved in play. Kenzie appeared to be joyfully content with solitary play and there was a definite change to his body language when Liam joined him. This event seems to support the concerns raised as Kenzie refused to answer Liam and preferred not to make any eye contact.

Observation 2

Name of the observer: Emily (EYP)
Name of the child: Kenzie, 4 years and 11 months
Date of observation: 09/07/11
Starting time: 11:40
Finishing time: 11:45
No. of adults present: 1 adult
Area of observation: writing area

Description of the activity observed:

Kenzie is sitting at a table with three other children. There is a tub of wax crayons close to him on the table and he has a picture of a lollipop lady in front of him which he has been asked to colour in. He is looking down at his lollipop lady picture and his tongue is moving from side to side as he holds a red wax crayon to the paper. Toby says to Kenzie: 'I need a green, can I have a green crayon?'. Kenzie remains silent and lifts his head to face Toby. Kenzie reaches out his left arm towards the tub of crayons, scoops the tub in the crook of his arm and pulls it towards his body. His eyebrows are lowered and his lips are puckered tightly.

Additional comments:

Kenzie is choosing not to communicate with Toby. He is capable of expressing himself and could well have asked Toby to wait until he had finished with the green crayon and put it back into the tub or give it to Toby. He does not want to share (something that he did earlier in the sand area as well). He makes eye contact on this occasion.

Observation 3

Name of the observer: Emily (EYP)
Name of the child: Kenzie, 4 years and 11 months
Date of observation: 11/07/11
Starting time: 11:15
Finishing time: 11:20
No. of adults present: 1 adult
Area of observation: outdoors play

Description of the activity observed:

During outdoor free play, Kenzie is sitting on a tricycle. He is pedalling, raising his head and 'La-La-ing' a tune loudly. Tommy and Claire run over to Kenzie and Tommy shouts excitedly, 'We are playing trains! Come and make a big, long train'. Kenzie stops pedalling and whilst Tommy is talking, Kenzie is looking and smiling at Tommy, as he is getting off the tricycle. Both of his arms are up in the air and he is shouting, 'Yeah, big train, yeah!' The three children run off together and form a line by standing one behind the other. They are all running around in a line, laughing and making: 'Woo-hoo' noises.

Additional comments:

Since the last observations, it appears that there is progress in terms of making friendships. Other members of staff report that he seems to have settled in well and engages in most activities. He has a lot of free play with Tommy. He has even started to bring items to the Show and Tell time at the beginning of the morning session, which also demonstrates an important social step forward.

In your early years setting, undertake at least three participant observations. Share your observations with a more experienced colleague or a fellow student. Was it difficult to find time to observe events and, if so, how did you overcome this?

Remember:

- *be factual and objective;*

- *record when and where it happened;*

- *record what was said and done;*

- *record facial expressions, body language, tones of voice, gestures.*

Non-participant observation (structured)

This type of observation is systematic and requires a number of techniques as described below. Non-participant observation requires the professional to step outside the role of practitioner – and not be involved in interacting with the children – acting instead as an objective observer of the child or an activity.

Preparation and organisation are required for non-participant observation and it needs to be planned in advance. It is statutory within the EYFS to provide a profile in the form of a portfolio for each child at the end of the EYFS:

> *In the final term of the year in which the child reaches age five, and no later than 30 June in that term, the EYFS Profile must be completed for each child. The Profile provides parents and carers, practitioners and teachers with a well-rounded picture of a child's knowledge, understanding and abilities, their progress against expected levels, and their readiness for Year 1. The Profile must reflect: ongoing observation; all relevant records held by the setting; discussions with parents and carers, and any other adults whom the teacher, parent or carer judges can offer a useful contribution.*

> *Each child's level of development must be assessed against the early learning goals. Practitioners must indicate whether children are meeting expected levels of development, or if they are exceeding expected levels, or not yet reaching expected levels ('emerging'). This is the EYFS Profile.*

> (DfE, 2012a, page 11)

For the early years professional to be able to meet the requirements of the EYFS and be able to complete the EYFSP, a systematic preparation towards this type of observation is crucial. The following sections aim to offer a detailed account of all different types of non-participant observation techniques available to early years workforce.

Preparing for non-participant observation

To become a systematic observer of children, you must first step out of the role you normally hold. Once you have decided when your observations will take place, you must withdraw from your role in the class and take on instead the role of the systematic observer. You should position yourself close to what you want to observe, but not interfere with the child/children in question or with the activity you are observing. Your presence as an observer should be discreet. You must not announce to the children that you are doing an observation and the children should be left alone. If children have been involved in the observation planning then there is no need to announce this each time. Sit closely, however, so that you can see and hear what happens. However, if a child interrupts your observation, it is better to stop rather than gather patchy and inaccurate information.

The best time to undertake observations will be determined by the aims and objectives. For example, an investigation of activities popular with children on arrival will be conducted. If you wish to observe children's language development, this could be done through a variety of observations at different times of the day.

Similarly, the type of activity to be observed should relate to your aims and objectives. You may, for example, wish to investigate the social interactions of a child during story time.

However, there will be cases where the type of activity to be observed is not always implicit in your aims and objectives. For example, your aim could be to observe social skills and your objective is to investigate whether or not the child in question forms good relationships with peers. In these instances it is important to refer back to the initial team meetings and reconsider the planning notes.

Preparation of the observations is crucial as it speeds up this process. The systematic way of recording your observations will become effective as you categorise, file, retrieve and then analyse them.

The observation techniques are explained in the following sections and include an evaluation of each one.

Written observations or narratives

This is the most common observation technique used by early years professionals and practitioners. It is a written record of an event as it occurs. The usual process is for observers to remove themselves from the activity, and observe from a discreet distance, avoiding interacting with or interrupting the children or the activities. Each observation is brief (no more than five minutes) and requires an accurate recording of exactly what happens at the time. This is written in the present tense. As discussed in the participant observation section, it is helpful to have forms already prepared. Again, these will include:

Name of the observer: _____

Name of the child: _____

Date of observation: _____

Starting time: _____   Finishing time: _____

No. of adults present: _____

Area of observation: _____

Description of the activity observed. _____

Additional comments: _____

I think _____ (In this section you add your thoughts that occurred during the observation, that they might help you later to interpret your recordings.)

It is helpful to add comments immediately after the observation has been completed, but care should be taken not to include any of your own comments during the observation itself. It is worth reiterating that observations should only include what *actually* occurs. Initial thoughts about what has been observed will give a good basis for later interpretation and analysis.

ACTIVITY 3

Look at the following photographs and write down what you have observed.

Share your recordings with a fellow student or a more experienced colleague. Have you recorded the same information?

Figure 3.1   Children drawing

Figure 3.2   Children playing

CASE STUDY

Name of child/children: Vicky
No. of adults present: 1
No. of children present: 2
Activity: cooking
Area: writing area
Date of observation: 04/02/12
Start time of observation: 13:45
Finishing time of observation: 13:50
Aim: Social development
Objective: To what extent Vicky has developed her ability to play successfully with others
Observation:
Two children (Vicky & Zara) and the early years professional (Maria) are in the writing area and they write down a recipe on a sheet of poster paper.

Maria: *So, we need one glass of olive oil and do you remember what else we wrote?*
Zara: *Sugar?*
Maria: *Can you remember how many glasses of sugar we need?*
Vicky: *Three and four glasses of that . . .* [she points to the water]
Maria: [pointing to the word 'water'] *Here, it says 'water'. We need four glasses of water.*
Maria: *What else did we say?*
Vicky: *Two glasses of that.*
Maria: *What is it?*

Vicky: I don't know.
Zara: *Is this semolina?*
Vicky: . . . *semolina.*
Maria: *And how many glasses of semolina do we need?*
Vicky: . . .*two?*
Zara: *Where does this say 'two'?*
Vicky: [points to the poster] *Here.*
Maria: *Yes. If you look here, we need two glasses of semolina.*

Comment: (a brief comment may be added here).
The children were working together with Maria in order to make sense of the recipe. Zara was helping Vicky, and with the help of the practitioner, they were trying to cook. The children show some evidence of working together towards a common purpose.

Evaluation of written observations

As this is an unstructured observation, the observer records anything and everything that happens (such as dialogues, movements, emotions) and this offers rich evidence of the children's behaviours or the implementation of activities. Some advantages of this technique are that the recordings are:

- accurate;

- complete;

- comprehensive.

However, as the observation proceeds, the information recorded can be taken out of context and is open to biased and inaccurate interpretations. A further disadvantage is that the observer may have omitted some relevant information, thus presenting an incomplete and patchy picture of the event. In a busy environment, where the observer is an integral part of the team, it may not always be possible or practical to release the team member in order to undertake an uninterrupted observation.

In your early years setting, undertake at least three written observations. Set clear aims and objectives for undertaking these. Be clear with yourself at what point of the day you anticipate undertaking them.

Evaluate the process, for example:

- *Have I included all the relevant information and details?*

- *Have I included any judgements or comments?*

- *Could I have missed significant events?*

Rating scales

Rating scales can be a valid technique for recording certain behaviour or aspects of development. This is a helpful technique as each behaviour is rated on a scale of a continuum from the lowest to highest (or vice versa) and it is marked against certain points along the scale. The observer makes a judgement about where on the scale a child's behaviour is. The most common rating scales in early years settings are the Ferre Laevers scales of involvement and well-being, as will be explained later in this section. There are two main types of rating scales: graphic and numerical. These scales are simple to make. Firstly you should identify the behaviour you want to observe, then you draw a line and mark off a number of interval points along the line. Normally we use five interval points. Although creating rating scales is a simple technique, the observer should know the children very well in order to be able to make judgements and to interpret children's behaviours. This technique can be used by children as well, if it is designed in a way that children have participated in the designing process so that they too fully understand. Children are normally the best judges of their behaviours if they are given the opportunity to express themselves.

Examples:
Graphic scale
Aim: Social development
Objective: Children wait for their turn during play

Always: Child always waits for his/her turn Often: Child often waits for his/her turn Sometimes: Child sometimes waits for his/her turn Rare: Child rarely waits for his/her turn Never: Child never waits for his/her turn

So you can have the following graphic scale for one child :

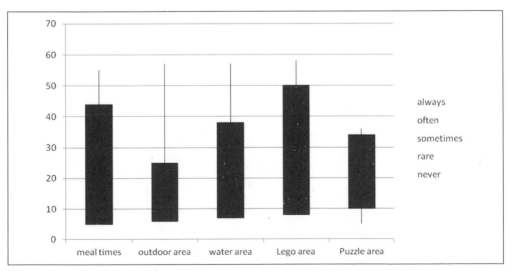

Figure 3.3 Child waits for his/her turn

Alternatively a child self-observation graphic scale can look like this:

ᵻᵻᵻᵻ   Objective: Wait for my turn

☺   always

😐   often

⧖   sometimes

🕐   rare

☹   never

It is important that these symbols would be very carefully explained to children before their use.

Numerical scales

These are normally used where certain behaviours or aspects of development are scored. For example, if you want to investigate children's feelings towards a certain activity, this can be done numerically.

☺   This activity made me happy (smiley face scores high: 10)

😐   This activity was OK (smiley face scores medium: 6)

☹   This activity did not interest me (scores low: 1)

Again these symbols would be very carefully explained to children prior to use.

Using this information, you can obtain an overall picture (in bar chart form) of whether children liked a certain activity:

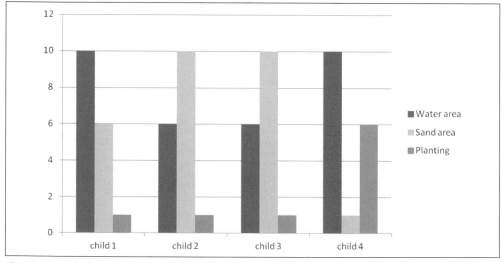

Figure 3.4 Activities children liked during the day

A commonly used and popular type of rating scale is the Ferre Laevers scale of well-being and involvement (Laevers, 1997, 1998, 1999, 2000). The work of Ferre Laevers is concerned with the question of quality in early years education. In an attempt to understand what makes an educational setting a quality one, he proposes that the activities offered and the children's involvement in the activities are key factors of quality. Consequently, along with Moons, he has developed rating scales for well-being and involvement around Ten Action Points, as an inventory of ten types of initiatives that will between them measure these two factors (Laevers and Moons, 1997).

The Leuven Scale for well-being

Signals:

1 Extremely low
The child clearly shows signs of discomfort such as crying or screaming. He or she may look dejected, sad, frightened or angry. The child does not respond to the environment, avoids contact and is withdrawn. The child may behave aggressively, hurting him/herself or others.

2 Low
The posture, facial expression and actions indicate that the child does not feel at ease. However, the signals are less explicit than for level 1 – or the sense of discomfort is not expressed the whole time.

3 Moderate
The child has a neutral posture. Facial expression and posture show little or no emotion. There are no signs indicating sadness or pleasure, comfort or discomfort.

4 High
The child shows obvious signs of satisfaction (as listed under level 5). However, these signals are not constantly present with the same intensity.

5 Extremely high
The child looks happy and cheerful, smiles, cries out with pleasure. He or she may be lively and full of energy. Actions can be spontaneous and expressive. The child may talk to him/herself, play with sounds, hum, sing. The child appears relaxed and does not show any signs of stress or tension. He or she is open and accessible to the environment. The child expresses self-confidence and self-assurance.

The Leuven Scale for involvement

Signals:

1 Extremely low
Activity is simple, repetitive and passive. The child seems absent and displays no energy. He or she may stare into space or look around to see what others are doing.

---

2 Low

Frequently interrupted activity. The child will be engaged in the activity for some of the time he or she is observed, but there will be moments of non-activity when the child will stare into space or be distracted by what is going on around him or her.

3 Moderate

Mainly continuous activity. The child is busy with the activity but at a fairly routine level and there are few signs of real involvement. He or she makes some progress with what he or she is doing but does not show much energy and concentration and can be easily distracted.

4 High

Continuous activity with intense moments. The child's activity has intense moments and at all times he or she seems involved. He or she is not easily distracted.

5 Extremely high

The child shows continuous and intense activity revealing the greatest involvement. He or she is concentrated, creative, energetic and persistent throughout nearly all the observed period.

Adapted from Laevers (1994, 2005 and 2009); Laevers and Moons (1997); Laevers, Bogaerts and Moons (1997).

Adapted by Ferre Laevers (ed.) Well-Being and Involvement in Care Settings. A Process-oriented Self-evaluation Instrument Research Centre for Experiential Education. Leuven, Belgium: Leuven University.

Checklists

Checklists are a very useful observation technique. It is a relatively difficult technique compared to narratives, as careful planning and preparation are required. Checklists can be used to record the activities of a single child or a group of children. They can also be used to record the progress of an activity for evaluation purposes. They are a useful tool for the early years professional, offering specific information and providing a starting point for planning activities for individuals or for groups of children.

The EYFS assessment scales provide a helpful starting point in creating a checklist. However, they cannot stand as an independent comprehensive checklist and should not be used as such, so they need to be developed further. The assessment scales in the EYFS can become objectives of your checklists but not the checklists themselves (see discussion on aims and objectives in Chapter 2).

Designing a checklist is not an easy task. Things to keep in mind when you create one include:

- length – keep it short;
- include items that are representative of the particular behaviour under study;
- include items that are representative of the age of the children you are observing;
- ensure that it can be understood by the whole team.

Example

Look at the checklist below, which attempts to record a child's behaviour during storytelling time.

- Which of the items below capture listening behaviours?
- Are there any additional items to be added to the list?
- In what ways is this a useful tool for the early years workforce?

> Name of Child:
>
> Date:
>
> No. of adults present:
>
> No. of children present:
>
> Activity: Story time
>
> Area: carpet
>
> Aim: Language development
>
> Objective: Listens and responds
>
> 1. Looks at teacher directly
>
> 2. Child pays attention
>
> 3. Facial movements:
>
> 3a) Smile
>
> 3b) Impressed
>
> 3c) Apathetic
>
> 4. Uses body language:
>
> 4a) Movement
>
> 4b) Direction
>
> 4c) Emotion
>
> 4d) Relaxation

4e) Interest

5. Asks questions

6. Joins in discussion

7. Answers questions

8. Predicts events from the book

Using the EYFS learning goals as your guide, create a checklist for social development. How are you going to tackle in your checklist the objective works as part of a group or class by taking turns and showing sharing fairly? Consider the timing of your observation and specific items to include in your checklist.

In the literature, a key element on observation process and planning is children's participation. The early years workforce needs not only to involve children in the process of observation planning but also to involve them in the actual observations. As illustrated in Chapter 2, the Mosaic approach has demonstrated a way of involving children in the observation process, but by using videos and cameras.

Involving children like this can be done in two ways: self-observation and observing others. In both cases, a number of observation techniques (see theory box) are available. Self-observation by children provides a way of recording in detail children's views and opinions about themselves. A number of techniques can be used, for example, drawings, digital media, photographs, videos, sketches made by children. However, if the techniques are designed in a way that is accessible to children, they are capable of using a number of observation techniques as will be demonstrated in the sections below through examples and case studies.

Checklists can become a useful tool for children who use them for self-observation, if they are developed in collaboration with the children.

CASE STUDY

Pictographic checklist

Aim: To assess children's social development during free play

Objective: Interactions during outdoor play

Social play	Pictographic presentation of items	Child self-evaluation
Prefer to watch others when they play		
Prefer to play on my own		
Prefer to have my own toys		✓
Prefer to play with others		✓
Prefer to join in when others have organised the play		
Prefer to be part of organising the play		✓
Prefer to share toys		✓

Table 3.2 Child self-evaluation checklist

Note: When pictographic lists are developed to be used by children, all images need to be very carefully explained to them.

Evaluation of checklists

Observation checklists can be quick, easy and efficient tools if they are carefully constructed. Checklists can be re-used and adapted – gaps in the checklist may be identified, children may demonstrate unanticipated behaviour, or the setting may have particular needs to be incorporated into it. Observation checklists can be used discreetly when the child is present. A number of different observers can use the same checklist to ensure that the information gathered is consistent, accurate and reliable. However, no checklists will be comprehensive and they should always be subject to additions and modifications. Finally, they can become a participatory tool for children to observe either themselves or others, so it increases the participation of children in the daily life and routines of the early years setting.

A major disadvantage of using a checklist is that, if an unforeseen event occurs during an observation, an important piece of information about a child or an activity may not have been covered by it. As this method requires knowledge of and expertise in child development, the participation of children and parents in its preparation may be limited. Although checklists provide a breadth of information, they may lack a depth of detail. It may be best to use them in conjunction with other techniques, to ensure that enough information is gathered.

Diagrammatic

This is a focused and purpose-specific observation technique and it includes a number of different methods:

- tracking;
- the use of sociograms;
- the use of histograms;
- the use of bar charts and pie charts.

Tracking

Tracking is used to record the amount of time a child spends on an activity of their choice or an activity that they have been asked to do. It does not explain *why* a child spends time on an activity or what a child did – it focuses only on time.

It is a useful tool when you want to:

- observe children's attention span;
- investigate the play areas preferred by children;
- assess how many times children visit an area;
- keep track of the use of different areas within the classroom.

Tracking can offer quantitative evidence of the above. However, it does not help you to explain why a particular behaviour has occurred. For example, you may want to observe

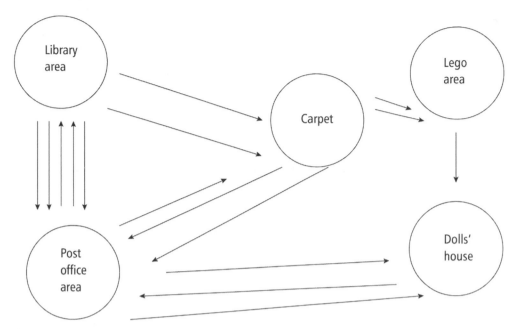

Figure 3.5   Diagram of tracking technique

the physical development of children, so you can use tracking to investigate in what ways children are active during the day. You can track where they go (e.g. tunnel area, playground etc). Children can participate actively in this. For example, in each area you can put a sack and different coloured stones or Lego pieces. Children each have their own colours and when they are using an area they add their coloured stone or Lego piece into the sack. At the end of the day you can count how many times a child has used each area. However, there is always the risk that children might forget to do this or are not putting more than one stone or Lego piece in each time, so early years practitioners or professionals should monitor this during the day.

Example

You are planning to change the learning areas of your class. You want to investigate which areas are the most popular among the children during free play so that you can enrich these. Areas not used by the children can subsequently be removed or replaced. You plan to carry out observations for one week and you are going to use tracking to do this. On completion, the findings show that the Lego area was the least popular among the children, so you decide to alter this area and enrich it with other construction materials instead (see Figure 3.5).

Sociogram

The focus of this technique is social development. It is a helpful tool to investigate how children interact with others during the day. It investigates the child's relationships with other children or adults and can demonstrate the child's popularity with other children.

Table 3.3   Examples of the sociogram technique

Children	Gregory	Alison	Gren	Raj
John	☺	☺	☺	☹
Katie	☺	☺	☺	☺
Mathew	☺	☹	☺	☺
Eric	☺	☺	☺	☺
George	☹	☺	☺	☺
Ahmed	☺	☺	☺	☺
Alia	☺	☹	☹	☹

The main advantage of this technique is that it speeds up the process of observing social development. However, in the same way as tracking, it does not explain the reasons *why* something happens, and can only tell us *what* happens. Sociograms can also offer misleading information as children's relationships can rapidly change.

Example:

The aim of the observation is to investigate how children form relationships with adults and peers. The specific objective is to investigate which children have formed smaller groups of friendships within the bigger class group. You show children three pictures: a smiley face, a sad face and a neutral face. The children are then asked to choose a picture that describes how they feel when they play with other children.

ACTIVITY 6

From this sociogram, can you make any interpretations?

Can you identify which child has most friends among the children that were asked?

Can you identify which child has the least friendships among the children that were asked?

Histograms

Histograms are a helpful technique to follow the development of a child for a long period of time. Histograms are a special form of bar chart where the information gathered is represented continuously rather than in discrete categories. This means that in a histogram there are not gaps between the columns representing the different categories. The main advantage of histograms is that you focus on a child's particular behaviour over a longer period of time.

CASE STUDY

Alia, aged two years and three months, has been finding it difficult to adapt to life in her early years classroom. A month after joining the class, she is still crying every day and asks for her mother. The early years practitioners have decided to observe her over a period of time to discover those times when she cries the most.

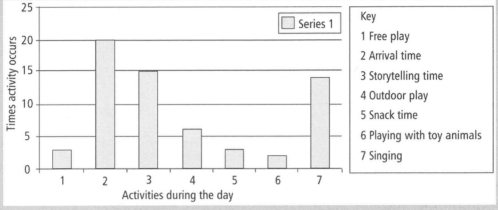

Figure 3.6 Histogram of adaptation to life in early years classroom

Bar charts and pie charts

These can both be useful as techniques for collecting information about both groups of and individual children. They can be produced to offer a visual presentation of the results from your observation recordings – how children come to the early years setting, for example. Others might include what children eat in school, which areas boys prefer using during the day, which areas girls prefer during the day, or what boys do during outdoor play.

CASE STUDY

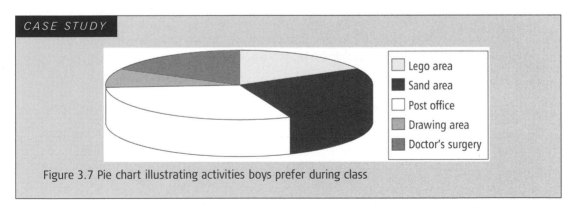

Figure 3.7 Pie chart illustrating activities boys prefer during class

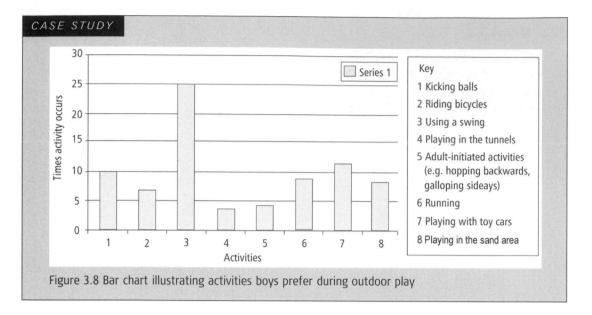

Figure 3.8 Bar chart illustrating activities boys prefer during outdoor play

Sampling

The aim of sampling is to identify how and when a particular behaviour occurs. The emphasis of sampling is on the duration of a particular behaviour. For example, you may want to investigate how long a two and a half-year-old child pays attention and focuses on storytelling or how often a three-year-old visits the sand area.

Time sampling

The observer records whether or not certain behaviours occur over a period of time. The focus of time sampling is on the duration of a particular behaviour. As time sampling records behaviours over a period of time, the frequency of the chosen behaviour is highlighted.

The main advantages of time sampling are:

- it takes less time and effort than other techniques;
- it helps you to remain objective as you know the behaviour that you are looking for;
- you can collect data on a number of children or a number for behaviours at the same time, and it provides information at intervals throughout a given period of time;
- it shows the frequency of behaviour.

However, time sampling is not open-ended. You may miss important behaviours as you are merely recording their frequency and not actually describing the behaviour. Time sampling is thus limited to observable behaviours that occur frequently. This usually focuses on a type of behaviour and may therefore give a skewed view of the behaviour of a child.

There are concerns that Val demonstrates some aggressive behaviour. The early years practitioners have decided to observe her, in order to find out how frequently Val demonstrates inappropriate behaviours that caused some distress among other children.

In preparing for the time sampling, it is important to define what inappropriate behaviour is. So the EYP, with reference to the EYFS, highlights some specific behaviours that can be easily observed and measured:

1. turn-taking;

2. taking toys from other children before they have finished with them;

3. hitting other children;

4. pushing other children;

5. shouting at other children.

To make the process faster, you can give a key to your chosen items. For example, you can use numbers or you can use the first letter of each item. It is up to you to decide how best you are going to code your items. Then you will need to decide when to record them – for example, departure time, outdoor play, literacy activities, etc. The emphasis on this observation is to record *when* Val demonstrates inappropriate behaviour.

Activity	Time	Behaviour observed
Departure time	8:45 a.m. 9:15 a.m.	1 4 5 2 3
Outdoor play	11:15 a.m. 2:20 p.m.	5 5 4 3 3 3 1
Storytelling	10:30 a.m.	1 3
Drawing area	3:00 p.m.	3 5 4 2 2
Dancing activity	11:45 a.m.	4 4 4 4 4 5

Table 3.4   Example of time sampling technique

Event sampling

The observer records a specific, pre-selected behaviour. Event sampling is used to study the conditions under which particular behaviours occur. It may be important to learn what triggers a particular kind of behaviour, e.g. biting.

Event sampling helps you to keep the event of the behaviour intact. This can make analysis easier and is objective, as behaviour can be defined ahead of time. It is also helpful to record infrequent behaviours. However, it can take the event out of context and, as it looks at specific behaviours, it can be lacking in detail.

CASE STUDY

Behaviours	Departure time	Outdoors play	Storytelling time	Gardening activities
Turn taking	**	*		****
Hits other children	****	********	****	***
Pushes other children	*******	*****		**
Shouts at other children	*	****		*

Table 3.5   Example of event sampling technique

Event sampling can help you to investigate what behaviours occur during different times of the day and with time sampling it is possible to determine how many times that occurs. In this way, you can develop strategies to either encourage certain behaviours or discourage others.

Digital media

With a variety of accessible electronic media now widely available, the early years team can use a number of techniques to improve the observation process. The digital camera or the digital video recorder can be used to add another dimension. The photographic evidence or tape/video recording evidence cannot replace the traditional observation techniques such as narratives, checklists sampling and diagrammatic methods, but they can be used as additional tools in the observation process. They offer accurate information about events as they capture everything objectively. The Mosaic approach (mentioned in Chapter 2) provides an excellent example of how media techniques were used as a useful method of gathering information about children's progress through the activities. In the Mosaic approach, it was demonstrated how media techniques became a powerful tool to encourage children's participation in contributing to data collection. They adopted media techniques as *participatory techniques* for use with children to enable them to be actively involved in the observation process (Clark and Moss, 2001).

However, when using digital techniques, we might want to consider that, for some children and early years practitioners, photographs or videos can make the observation intrusive as they might object to being photographed or videoed. It also eliminates the anonymity and confidentiality factor and might affect behaviour, and spontaneity might be lost. It is also worth mentioning that digital media for observation serve as representation of a narrative and we cannot ignore the fact that that they illustrate a narrative sequence; their interpretation is subject to individual experiences. Pink addresses this in the following extract:

> [. . .] visual research methods [in our case visual observation techniques] are not purely visual. Rather they pay a particular attention to visual aspects of culture. Similarly, they cannot be used independently of other methods; neither a purely visual ethnography nor an exclusively visual approach to culture exist.

(2007, page 21)

Try to evaluate the different observation techniques. Your evaluations should aim to answer the following questions:

1. *Does this observation technique help me to gain rich information in order to investigate/answer my specific observation aim/focus/objective?*

2. *What are the advantages of using this technique? (They always need to be linked with your observation aim/objective/focus.)*

3. *What are the disadvantages of using this technique? (Again, they must be linked with your observation aim/objective/focus.)*

SUMMARY

This chapter discussed the most common tools that the early years workforce can use to observe children and to evaluate the education programme and its activities. The two dominant observation methods are participatory observation and non-participatory observation. The non-participatory observations include:

- *written observation;*

- *rating scales;*

- *checklists;*

- *diagrammatic observation;*

- *sampling.*

The next chapter aims to discuss how we record and analyse observations

FURTHER
READING

For extensive examples on observation techniques, see the work of:

Riddall-Leech, S (2008) *How to observe children* (2nd ed.). Oxford: Heinemann Educational Publishers.

Salaman, A and Tutchell, S (2005) *Planning educational visits for the early years.* London: SAGE.

Smidt, S. (2005) *Observing, assessing and planning for children in the early years.* London: Routledge.

4 Analysing and documenting observations

Through reading this chapter, you should:

- understand the analysis process of the observation recordings;
- distinguish between a valid and faulty explanation of observation recordings;
- understand the importance of documenting your observation recordings;
- explore different ways of documenting your evidence.

Analysing and documenting observations is an essential aspect of observation planning. Each early years team should find their own ways to document the observation findings that are meaningful to their context.

Introduction

This chapter aims to discuss the final step in observation planning. So far we have discussed the purpose of observation, addressing key issues of team, parental and child involvement, as well as the importance of clear aims and objectives. Issues around objectives have been addressed. Chapter 3 discussed in detail the observation techniques available in order to gather evidence. The next step is analysis of the recordings and documentation – and this is explored in the following sections.

Analysing observations

Once information has been collected, there is a need to analyse the findings. This is a process where all the team needs to get involved and participate. All the data from the observations will be processed during the analysis in order to have a complete picture of either the child under focus or of the education programme.

Analysis is a very difficult part of the process. It requires objectivity and careful consideration of all the facts, in order to offer an accurate portrait for each child and an accurate evaluation of the educational programme.

In order to interpret your observation, and whilst examining its collection, it is important that the recordings are read thoroughly. The next step is to investigate whether there is any interpretation that can be applied to the specific event that you have recorded. Early years professionals and practitioners are busy people. They have to look after the children and implement the EYFS, so during the hectic pace and workload of the day, they may have collected data without attempting any interpretation of them. Once an observation has been conducted, an analysis must be performed as soon as possible thereafter. Memory deteriorates with time . . .

Analysing

Valid explanation: can a possible explanation be derived from the behaviour you have observed?

Faulty explanation (or biased): can a possible explanation be derived from your personal opinion?

Conclusions: is a judgement based on valid explanations made from accumulated observation recordings?

A valid explanation is one where it is possible to reach a conclusion derived from the behaviour recorded. These explanations should not be biased and should not be derived from personal opinions.

Observation recording: *Vicky would not let Kelly borrow her orange pencil.*

A valid and accurate explanation may be one that says:

- Vicky had not finished using her pencil so she did not give it to Kelly.
- A biased or faulty explanation may be the one that says:
- Vicky does not know how to share.

In the above example we do not have enough evidence to support whether Vicky wanted to share or not, so making such an interpretation would be based on our personal knowledge of Vicky as a child, and not from the recorded observation.

It is easy to draw an inappropriate conclusion on the basis of the evidence. During the process, observers must take immediate decisions about what to record, so the results may be superficial or form an unreliable account and there is no chance of an exact repeat of the behaviour. Often, faulty conclusions can also be made when information about prior activities cannot be obtained. Therefore, it is helpful for observations to be repeated either by another person or at different times during the day or on different days, so that reliability can be checked.

ACTIVITY 1

Look at the photo of the boy (George) and write down what you see:

Figure 4.1 Boy on a bike

Is your observation recording similar to this?

Observation recording: George is sitting on the bike.

Here are two explanations:

1. George can ride a bike.

2. George knows how to sit on a bike.

Which one is faulty and which one is valid? What conclusions can you validly draw?

Observations can provide highly accurate, detailed and verifiable information (Moore, 2001). However, as mentioned in Chapter 2, observations are susceptible to bias. This can occur either because of the observer's lack of attention to significant events, or because observers record something they thought they saw rather than what actually occurred (Simpson and Tunson, 1995). So the final step in the process of analysing observation recordings is how you arrive at conclusions. Conclusions should be based on a number of valid and accurate explanations of the observation recordings. In your conclusions you need more evidence to back up your final statement. As mentioned above, making conclusions is always the product of judgements that are made from a number of valid inferences of the observed event(s). For example, in the above case, if we had a number of different observation recordings that demonstrated that Vicky did not give any toys or objects to other children at different times of the day or during different activities, we could then conclude that Vicky does not know how to share.

Analysing your observations is an essential part of the process. In this, it is important that all the early years team is involved, as well as parents or carers. *The quality of the observations and of the analysis of these observations will determine the quality of assessment made* (Lally and Hurst 1992, page 79).

Lally and Hurst (1992) have developed a framework for analysing the recordings of the observations. They suggest a series of statements that will enable staff to start discussions around children's assessments.

- Acknowledge their previous experiences of the child and place observation in the context of this knowledge.

- Make use of their observations to inform their assessment record of the child.

- Raise further questions about the child's experiences. (These may be in connection with the role of the provision or of the involvement of other children or adults with the child. In this way, one observation can be seen to inspire further investigation.)

- Use the information to plan to support the child's future learning.

- Communicate with one another, as analysis of observations is shared (Lally and Hurst, 1992, page 90).

Obviously, when working within the EYFS you operate under a framework for assessment. This can be translated into a series of questions to start your analysis.

- What does this observation tell us about each child's experiences and progress?

- What does this observation tell us about each child's interests, skills, development and learning achievements?

- What information do you still need to assess each child fully in order to complete the EYFS Profile?

- How will this observation help you to share information with the children, parents, and other services in order to promote partnership?

- How will this observation help you to evaluate the implementation of your activities within EYFS?

- Has your observation met the aims and objectives of its design?

Prior to the completion of the assessment scales, there are steps to undertake in order to help you with the analysis of observation recordings. Firstly, having the development of the child as a guide, focus on an individual child and create a specific profile of his or her development. Within this framework, you can make comparisons as to what extent the child has met certain developmental areas, what the strengths of the child are, and where you need to focus more in order to enhance this child's development. For example, looking at a child's personal, emotional and social development, the EYFS assessment scales can become your criteria for investigating where this child is developmentally.

Consequently, with a mixture of observations providing cumulative data, you can begin to build a profile of the child's progress through the EYFS. This assists you to plan appropriate activities to support this child's development and learning.

Secondly, you can refer back to the aims of observations that reflect the learning goals of EYFS and try to compare your observation recordings alongside the aims of the learning goals. This will enable you to evaluate whether or not your activities have been implemented effectively, based on a child's progress.

Documenting observation findings

The final stage of observation planning is the documentation. Again, in this final stage, team, parental and child involvement are essential elements.

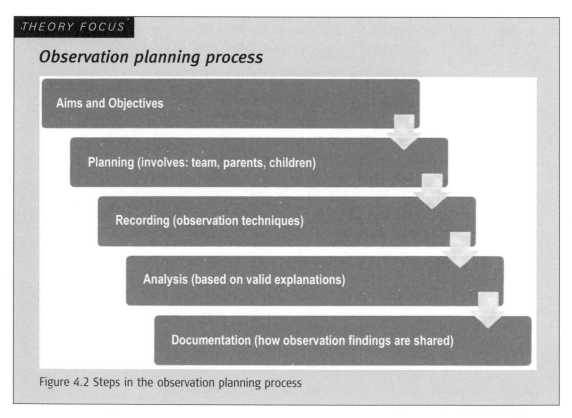

THEORY FOCUS

Observation planning process

Aims and Objectives

Planning (involves: team, parents, children)

Recording (observation techniques)

Analysis (based on valid explanations)

Documentation (how observation findings are shared)

Figure 4.2 Steps in the observation planning process

There is a plethora of different and inventive ways on how observation findings can be documented, as demonstrated in the following examples.

The Mosaic approach

The Mosaic project, as mentioned in Chapter 2, aimed to *emphasise that listening [to children] is an active process, involving not just hearing but interpreting, constructing meaning and responding* (Clark and Moss, 2001, page 7). Children were involved in the process of planning their own learning by listening to their own voices and by providing their own perspectives on their lives. The Mosaic approach aimed to enable them to *co-construct* the activities (Clark and Moss, 2001). In this study, the discussion of documentation was determined by creating a dialogue among children, practitioners, older children, parents and researchers. The involvement of all participants was central. Dialogue about the documentation was shared in the following ways:

The idea of creating portfolios as tools of documentation was introduced. These portfolios were open and new tools or materials could be added with the participation of adults, parents and children. Whenever children's or adults' skills and interests were developing, these were added to the portfolio. The important aspect of these portfolios was the data collection tools, developed to enable children to express their views, ideas and feelings (Clark and Moss, 2001). Observation recordings were central in the Mosaic approach. Child conferencing – which took the form of a short interview – and tours with the child, as well as photographs and videos, were the basis for collecting information around children's interests and skills. Thus, children's participation was central throughout the child-conferencing technique.

In order to create these portfolios, three important aspects were taken into consideration:

1. The tools used throughout the process of collecting information about children's perspectives of their own lives.

2. The view of the child as an 'expert' on his or her own life.

3. The involvement of all participants, especially parents and key workers, was highly valued.

As a result, the Mosaic approach suggested a new way of documenting the observation of children. Working in an educational setting, assessment for children should not only focus on the developmental and educational goals, but should start from the child's perspectives, and should also emphasise the child's life experiences.

Reflect on your own practice, which is underpinned by EYFS, and consider whether or not you can adopt some of the strategies of the Mosaic approach.

Will this be possible with the workload in your setting?

Will it promote children's and parents' participation? If yes, in what ways?

Te Whaariki and Learning Stories

Te Whaariki does not have a standardised approach to the documentation of observation recordings. Each setting decides to assess, and consequently document, observation recordings according to their own aims and objectives and according to the purpose of the assessment. Parents not only give their permission, but are also actively involved in the process.

Documentation in a Te Whaariki class involves: the observation findings, photographs, the transcripts of children's interactions either with their peers or with adults, and the children's own work. Ten reasons for documenting observation recording are described:

1. To understand children's learning better. Observations are looked at very carefully and the process of writing these observations helps the early years team to focus upon a child's development in order to understand it and its needs better.

2. To implement discussion of children's learning. Individual assessments are the starting point for a discussion of their learning.

3. It is a communication tool for sharing information with all the participants.

4. To assess how situations have been handled. The participation of adults and children enables the early years practitioners to reflect on their practice.

5. In planning learning models for individuals and groups, an emphasis on the central role of assessment is to determine whether or not the learning activities designed do have an effect on children's learning – and whether or not this learning is meeting their needs.

6. To ensure that all children receive attention. It is important to investigate if all children have the necessary attention so that no child misses either being seen or heard. In the early years class, some children tend to receive more attention than others, thus the Te Whaariki documentation attempts to ensure that all children share the same amount of consideration. Important tools for this are the *learning stories*, which enable early years practitioners to plan the development of positive interests and skills.

7. To highlight that learning is valued in the setting. Early years practitioners develop activities within the Te Whaariki curriculum. Documentation of observation enables practitioners to gain an insight into children's understanding of these values, and it is a way of directly involving children in the process, as children subsequently acquire an understanding of the meanings and purposes of the activities.

8. To involve children in self-assessment. Encouraging children to assess themselves helps the early years professional to enable them to take ownership of their own learning and to make choices of what work should go into their portfolios or files. However, it is acknowledged that self-evaluation of children can have its pitfalls, as

it can lead to lack of response in terms of spontaneity from children, and can increase an attitude towards performance-driven behaviours, rather than exploration (which is a central premise of Te Whaariki).

9. To involve the parents in a discussion of assessment. When families are informed, their input and involvement increase, and this can subsequently help to meet the outcomes of the education programme.

10. To share experiences with family. The *Learning Stories*, as a tool for sharing information, can not only make very interesting reading for the families, but also enables them to share what their children are doing when they are not with them.

ACTIVITY **3**

Reflecting on how the EYFS Assessment Scales are used, can you identify any of these purposes for observation in the practice in your setting?

CASE STUDY

Laevers' scales of involvement and well-being

As mentioned in Chapter 3, Ferre Laevers at the University of Leuven introduced the Scales of Involvement and Well-being in 1976. The instrument was developed at the Research Centre for Experiential Education (Leuven University, Belgium). The aim is that these scales measure and monitor children's involvement and engagement in activities as well as their well-being.

The scales aim to:

- serve as a tool for self-assessment by care settings;

- focus on quality, taking into consideration the child and its experience of the care environment;

- achieve appropriateness for the wide range of care provision.

There are three steps in the process:

Step 1 – assessment of the actual levels of well-being and involvement;

Step 2 – analysis of observations;

Step 3 – selection and implementation of actions to improve quality of practice in the early years setting.

This documentation process is mainly based on numerical evidence, interpreted by the team involved in the process.

Reggio Emilia: pedagogical documentation

Reggio Emilia is an alternative and flexible pedagogical approach to a pre-defined and pre-described curriculum, in which children, parents and teachers are working together through a variety of activities. Children express their ideas and lead the activities according to their interests. One of the main questions about the Reggio approach concerns the way in which children's making meaning can be assessed. The concept of pedagogical documentation in Reggio is a way of collecting children's experiences during activities through materials, photographs, videos, notes and audio recordings. This information becomes visible to others (children and parents) through exhibits, DVDs, books, posters and pamphlets. The teachers act as recorders/documenters for the children, helping them to revisit their actions and self-assess their learning. In the Reggio classroom documentation is an integral part of the procedure and it aims for a pedagogy in which children are listened to. Rinaldi stresses two important aspects of documenting children's activities:

1. [Documentation] . . . makes visible the nature of the learning process and strategies used by each child, and makes the subjective and inter-subjective process a common parsimony;

2. it enables reading, revisiting and assessment in time and in space and the actions become an integral part of the knowledge-building process (2005, page 23).

The most popular and frequently used method of documentation is the visual one. As seen in the Mosaic approach, Learning Stories from Te Whaariki and the pedagogical documentation of the Reggio Emilia approach, visual documentation seems to be the most appropriate way of recording observations. Using images, photos and videos is a good way of describing an activity or a behaviour and it makes it vivid and real. Visual documentation offers a direct representation of the daily life of the setting and at the same time is accessible to children of all ages as it *speaks* in a *visual language* that children of all ages can understand and narrate in their own words.

Reading photographs or videos is a direct and immediate tool of communication. However, as Wright reflects with scepticism, photographs *are only perceived as real by cultural convention: they only appear realistic because we have been taught to see them as such* (1990, page 6). It is important to be aware that, when photographs or videos are used to share observations, they still require interpretation as different people or different children will not 'see' images in the same way. As mentioned in Chapter 3, the use of digital media as a method for observation, is a way of selecting observation recordings and of reconstructing reality, but reality for each of us is perceived differently. Thus, when we try to interpret photographs or videos, we do need to look for indicators which might be ambiguous and then try to interpret what this meaning might indicate. The follow example illustrates this point:

Boys with weapons

Figure 4.3 Boys with weapons

When you attempt to 'read' a photograph or a video, you need to look at elements that convey meaning. It is helpful to distinguish between what you see and how you interpret what you see. So it is helpful to look for indicators in a photograph and what they might show.

Indicators	Indication
Child one (on left): holds the sword and the shield, looks straight at the camera. His lips are stressed, his right hand is pointing with the sword.	Feigns aggression, he is posing for the camera. Knows how to hold the shield and the sword.
Child with gun (on right): holds gun with both hands, points gun direction in front of him, his lips are relaxed, his eyes are looking at the end of the gun.	Pretends to shout, focuses on the pretend play of shouting.
Child with no toys in his hand (in the middle): his lips are sucked inside his mouth, his eyes are looking into the camera.	Poses for the camera, no interest in the weapons.
Child with bow and arrow (in the front): his left hand holds bow and arrow steady, right hand pulls the bow string back, his eyes look straight at the camera.	Feigns aggression. Poses for the camera, knows how to play with a bow and arrow.

Table 4.1   Indicators and indications in photo example 'Boys with weapons'

What other indicators can you see in the photograph (Figure 4.3? What meaning(s) might they indicate?

Try this process with a video observation.

To conclude, what each early years setting decides as a way to document observations, should be consistent, understood by all involved in the process (team, parents, children) and at the same time be accessible by all participants. It is essential that the documentation process should be the product of participation, shared amongst all involved, helpful, useful and focused on the aims and objectives of the planning process. It also needs to be practical and linked with the setting's curricular practices.

THEORY FOCUS

Effective documentation in practice
Adapted from Luff (2007)

Documentation should enhance our walks in the park with children and not prevent them happening. It is not necessary to record everything, to spend time producing masses of perfect paperwork which is filed away and rarely seen. It is important, however, to recognise that thinking and learning are not easily visible and that our memories are not unlimited. Writing down an observation, photocopying a drawing, or taking a photograph help us to bring learning into view, so that it can be seen, reflected upon and discussed. Three practical approaches to documentation are considered below. Any of these can be adapted, according to available resources, and used in a variety of early years settings.

Photo sequences
By taking a digital camera along to the park, staff may capture a sequence of photographs. These could be of a child gaining confidence on the climbing frame, or a small group of children finding and examining leaves and acorns. On returning to the nursery, even before these pictures are printed, children will love to sit with a practitioner and review the images on a computer screen (or, if available, via a data projector) recognising themselves, naming other children, remembering and talking about what they did on the walk. As soon as selected images are printed, they can be displayed in simple photograph albums or on the nursery walls, with or without captions. Children can then see and recall their actions, parents and visitors to the nursery have evidence of what happened during the walk in the park and may understand and comment on the learning that occurred, and the staff can use the pictures as a starting point of their discussions, evaluations and the planning of future outings.

Child profiles

A portfolio, or profile, compiled during a child's time during attending an early years setting can provide a very positive record of what that child can do and has achieved (Driscoll and Rudge, 2005). Kept in a scrapbook, document wallet or loose-leaf folder, such profiles might contain written observations, children's drawings and photographs of the child involved in activities. It is not possible or necessary to record everything in a profile but at key points during the child's time at nursery, as part of a process of regular occasional monitoring, on special occasions, or when something notable occurs, entries can be made. It is likely that a child's key worker will have the main responsibility for keeping the profile but will use it in an open and inclusive way, as an invaluable means of building relationships with the child and family and for creating and sustaining links between nursery and home. Children are proud of their profiles and can take decisions about what goes into them. They may want to include the leaf rubbing they did at the park, or the photograph of them pushing their friend on the swing. Parents are thrilled to see what their children are achieving at nursery and the profile can provide a stimulus to talk about what children are doing at home. The profile may be taken home and parents may add pictures or stories about family events. For parents, nursery staff and other professionals, the profile can be an invaluable document to review the child's strengths, understand their interests, and note the progress that has been made.

Learning Stories

Practitioners, parents and children can also all be involved in contributing to Learning Stories. As with photo sequences and portfolios, this approach focuses upon positive outcomes emphasising each child's participation and their development of positive dispositions and attitudes towards learning. Observations are made, often recorded on prepared pro-formas. These provide space for an observation, or Learning Story, to be recorded and have sections for a short-term review, which allows the practitioner to offer an initial interpretation of the Learning Story. The observed story is then discussed and interpreted collaboratively and, along with photographs, work samples and comments from the child and parents, becomes the basis for decisions about the next steps for learning (Carr 2001). In this approach, the focus is upon the child as a learner within the early years setting with the recognition that their learning is supported and enhanced by the people and resources which promote the child's activity and thinking. If a notebook and camera are taken on the walk to the park, a simple Learning Story can be captured: 'W. picked something up off the ground and said, "It's an acorn." He handed it to E. saying, "It's muddy. Can you get the mud off it?" When E. cleaned it and handed it back, he tried very hard to remove the shell from the acorn. He asked E. to break it open and then looked at the seed inside and said, "It's white."' Returning to the nursery, the short-term review may be that W. recognises the acorn and is curious to find out what's inside. Talking to other staff, to W. and his mother you may discover that W. is developing an interest in

THEORY FOCUS *continued*

finding natural objects and you then might plan to collect and examine more acorns, to bring them back to nursery to look at more closely, with a magnifying glass, and perhaps plant some acorns to investigate their growth.

Luff, P. (2007, pages 185–96) *Written observations or walks in the park: Documenting children's experiences,* in J. Moyles (Ed) *Early Years Foundations: Meeting the Challenge,* Maidenhead: Open University Press.

ACTIVITY 5

Reading the above extract, reflect on your own setting and discuss:

How much assessment is formally documented in your setting? Who has access to this documentation, and how? Is this type of documentation accessible to the parents and the children? What methods do you use to document your observations?

Limitations of observations

Throughout this book the value of observation in early years education has been emphasised. However, you need to be aware of the limitations, in the same way as any method or tool. One of the main limitations of observation is that capturing what actually happens or a certain behaviour or activity divorces it from its history. Using only observation as a method to collect evidence of children's development, behaviours, learning or to inform your planning, does not answer the key question of how the behaviour occurred, how the learning occurred, how the activities developed.

A key element in the development and behaviour of each child is his/her personal history and the culture in which that child has been brought up, any changes in the family structure (if any), the dynamics of the child's direct and indirect environment and the impact this may have had on the child's behaviour. We are all part of a community and its ecology (beliefs, customs, values, services, policies) and as such these aspects may not become apparent by visual observation alone. Such evidence on its own decontextualises the behaviour.

Thus it is important to use methods or techniques other than observation to gain a broader picture. This is an important limitation to consider and finding other ways of answering the question should also be found. Team meetings, parental involvement and child involvement are essential elements to minimise this limitation. These can offer information you are seeking, unavailable in the observation. In the analysis and documentation processes, it is important to consider the origins of what has been observed, cross-referencing with evidence from other sources. Gillham concludes that:

Observations cannot tell the whole story; and even when extended over time, it (sic) *can only incorporate a narrow section of evolution of a group, a culture or an individual.*

(2008, page 100)

Thus there is always a need for complementary methods.

SUMMARY

This chapter concludes the steps in observation planning. It discussed how observation recordings are analysed and how important it is to make valid explanations of the recordings in order to arrive at conclusions on what the observation recordings 'say' to us. It also discussed different documentation practices such as the Mosaic approach, Learning Stories and pedagogical documentation. All demonstrate how the observation process can be documented in a way which enables the participation of children and parents. There are also examples of how documentation can be used to share information with any individual interested in children's development and learning in an informal or formal way, the early years workforce and parents. Finally, a key limitation of observation was addressed – observation cannot be the only method in early years settings to collect evidence as it cannot tell the whole story. Thus, it is essential that observation planning is the outcome of team, parental and child involvement.

In the next chapter, the ethical implications of observation will be explored and how children can participate in both the planning process and in the observation itself will be discussed.

FURTHER READING

Carr, M (1998) *Assessing Children's Learning in Early Childhood Settings: A development programme for discussion and reflection.* Wellington: New Zealand Council for Educational Research.

Carr, M (2001) *Assessment in Early Childhood Settings.* London: Paul Chapman Publishing.

Clark, A and Moss, P (2001) *Listening to young children: The Mosaic approach.* London: National Children's Bureau.

Rinaldi, C (2006) *In dialogue with Reggio Emilia, Listening, researching and learning.* London: Routledge.

For more information on documentation with a particular focus on visual documentation:

Luff, P (2007) *Written observations or walks in the park: Documenting children's experiences,* in Moyles, J (Ed.) *Early Years Foundations: Meeting the Challenge.* Maidenhead: Open University Press.

WEBSITES

For information on learning journeys and Learning Stories you can access:
Pen Green Research, Development and Training Base and Leadership Centre
www.pengreen.org/pengreenresearch.php

5 Ethical implications

> Through reading this chapter, you should understand:
>
> - the ethical implications of observing young children;
>
> - the importance of team involvement;
>
> - the importance of child involvement;
>
> - the importance of parental involvement;
>
> - the role of the adult as a guardian of young children.
>
> Ethical practices need to be considered throughout the observation process in the early years setting. It will be argued that although consent is really valid, ethical practice observing young children is limited not only to consent but also involves a number of other issues.

Introduction

This chapter aims to discuss the ethical implications of observing young children. It will explain the role of the adult as a guardian of young children whilst data are being collected for assessment purposes. It will emphasise the fact that, before setting the task of observing children, careful consideration of their right to participate or not (Palaiologou, 2012b) should be made, along with the ethics involved in the process. It will also discuss the importance of reporting data about a child to other professionals and to parents in an ethical manner.

Ethics of the observation process

As emphasised in previous chapters, observations should maintain a central role within early years practice. This role is to promote the quality of care and education that children receive and to enhance professional practice. Observations help the early years team to extend their understanding about their educational programme, in addition to their understanding of the children themselves. In order to consider the ethical implications involved in observations, it is essential to consider their purpose.

Early years professionals and practitioners should create an ethical framework around any observation process which is going to inform planning education programmes and assessments of each child. The ethical guidelines for the early years environment should underpin the work of professionals. Ethical considerations involve consent from all involved in the process – children, parents, the professional team – and the extent to which any observation is needed (along with how records are kept and who will have access to them). The following paragraphs will discuss the ethical issues involved throughout the observation process.

Team involvement

Team involvement is the starting point. As explained in Chapter 2, the early years team meets and discusses the observation design, and the aims and objectives of the process. It is at this initial meeting that the creation of the ethical framework should occur. As part of this, the members of the team need to agree to a code of practice which will reflect on the aims and the purposes for observation. Mutual respect, the creation of a good working environment where all opinions are valued and where everyone's expertise, interests and skills are encouraged and taken into consideration, are elements in the creation of an ethical code between members of the team, where everyone feels safe, free and confident to be involved and which reflects the aims of the observation within the EYFS framework.

In your ethical considerations, the starting point is what information will be collected. This is important. Unnecessary collection of information on children or the educational programme should be avoided and/or limited. It is crucial for the observation process that the aims and objectives are well defined and explained. The aims and objectives of observations should not only be clarified, but also understood by all members of the early years team and agreed by all. All the team members should be able to express their views. The final result of the meeting is a decision on the observation processes, techniques and methods, and the observation design should be a collaborative product. The needs of the setting, as well as the needs of the children and the team members, should be met. These needs include:

- an agreement on the accessibility of the information;

- the filing and sharing among team members' observation recordings;

- how and who will share the information with the participants involved.

ACTIVITY 1

Consider in your setting whether or not there is a team meeting in place when observation processes are discussed and designed.

Parental involvement

One of the key procedures in establishing an ethical code is to gain parental involvement. The early years team has a challenging task, seeking not only parental consent but also parental involvement as well. Working in early years can be overwhelming as practitioners and professionals are busy implementing the curriculum, complying with legislation and delivering the learning goals of the EYFS. It is important that, despite the demands of the daily routine, the involvement of parents in the observation process is prioritised. So, parental involvement should not be limited to merely signing a consent form. Parents should be involved and participate when observations are designed as an integral part of the ethics of the observations.

The gathering of observational evidence is crucial for early years practice so that links can be made between the individual developmental needs, learning achievements, the planning of appropriate activities and the promotion of partnership. In such a context, parental involvement should be encouraged and parents should be invited to an in-depth discussion with the practitioners. When this happens, parents can provide collaboration throughout the process. Parents can become helpful co-operators in the observation process.

The aims and objectives of the process should be explained to the parents in a transparent and understandable manner. Emphasis should be placed on why observation is important in the daily practice of the early years, how it is going to benefit the education programme and furthermore how it will inform the activities designed for the children.

It is also central to explain to the parents that they can have access to the records at all times throughout the process. Parental involvement ought to be a choice for the parents and they should retain the right to withdraw their participation at any time.

A number of questions can help us to investigate the degree of parental involvement.

- Have the purposes of the observation process been explained to the parents?

- Have parents expressed their opinions and been allowed to make any suggestions or alterations?

- Have parents been reassured that they will be able to access the observation recordings as and when they wish?

- Are parents aware that they will be involved regularly and that they will remain informed about the observation process?

ACTIVITY **2**

Reflecting on your own setting, consider how parental involvement is obtained and what ethical procedures you have in place to involve parents.

The following points highlight the steps early years professionals should undertake to fulfil their responsibility for maintaining parental involvement. It is the responsibility of the early years professional to undertake steps to maintain parental involvement. These are to ensure that:

- parents are kept fully informed throughout the process;

- parents are involved whilst the child's assessment profile is being created;

- regular meetings with the parents are taking place to keep them informed and to gain their trust, commitment and to maintain their participation.

There is a necessity for a constant flow of information from the early years team, and not only during parents' evenings or in parents' meetings. A small note or a photograph explaining what the child has done during a day can be a good starting point for a short discussion but, at the same time, it is a valid tool for continuous communication with the parents

---

ACTIVITY 3

Study the Welfare Requirements section of EYFS and try to reflect on how you can maintain parental involvement within your own setting.

Children's involvement

The UN Convention on the Rights of the Child (UN, 1989) sets the standards for listening to children's voices and promoting children's involvement in any decision-making that involves them. Since the UN Convention, there has been an emphasis on children having an increased control over the policies, services and curricula that concerns them. As has already been explained, the ethics on observing children should apply to all participants in the process, and ought to apply throughout. Consequently, children need to be informed and have explained to them the purposes of any observation.

The question for early years practitioners is: at what age are children able to get involved in the process, and how can they be informed about the observation effectively? When babies and young children are observed, especially below the age of two years, it is more difficult and challenging to involve them due to the children's limited understanding. Their involvement will be different. Practitioners are not going to expect the babies and toddlers to voice their opinions. Practitioners can involve babies and toddlers by acknowledging that their emotions can be an indicator of their participation. For example, smiling or eye contact might be interpreted as babies and toddlers being comfortable with the observation taking place. Practitioners should treat babies and toddlers with sensitivity, being aware and responsive to behaviours that might indicate that they do not wish to participate.

However, as children grow older and more aware (say, at around the age of three) the early years professional and practitioner can seek to involve the children in the observation process. Play can become the best context for this and can be a tool to seek consent and involvement from very young children. Role-play, and children's drawing and story time, can provide a helpful context for a child's involvement. For example, children can create a story about their feelings with regards to a certain activity and they can illustrate this story with their own drawings. In Chapter 3 it was demonstrated that some methods can be used by children if they are designed in a way that are understood by them (see examples of rating scales and checklists in Chapter 3). A number of innovative approaches (see Clark and Moss, 2001, pedagogical documentation in Chapter 4) have shown us ways in which children can actively participate in the observation process. However, central to ethical practice should be the questions '*How do we act with children?*' and '*How do we respect children's wishes to participate but equally not to participate?*' (Palaiologou, 2012b) in the observation process.

There are further advantages to child involvement, aside from its ethical value alone. When children have been made aware that observations take place, it aids the professional in stepping back and becoming a systematic observer. When children are aware that this will happen, they are less likely to disturb this process. In addition, they know where to go when they need something. In this way, your role as an observer becomes easier and more effective. Moreover, children can participate, and from a very young age they can start taking control of the processes that involve them.

ACTIVITY **4**

1. *Think how you can involve toddlers (say at around the age of 16 months) when you try to observe how they use their first language to interact with other children or adults.*

2. *Think how you can involve children (say at around the age of 26 months) when you try to discover why a child in a class does not take turns and does not want to share.*

To summarise, ethical considerations should not be separate from the observation process but an integral part of it. Ethical considerations should underpin the whole of the observation process. Parental involvement, as well as child involvement, should not be limited to informed consent forms. Parents and children should be invited into the process of observation and play an active role within it.

ACTIVITY **5**

The following list of questions can be used to check whether or not the ethics have been applied in the observation process.

- *Has the whole team agreed with the aims and objectives of the observation process?*

- *Has the whole team agreed with the observation methods and techniques?*

- *Have the parents been informed – and has the observation process been fully explained to them?*

- *Have the nature of the observations (including aims, objectives and what tools will be used) been explained to the children (where applicable)?*

- *Have you made clear that all members concerned in the observation will have access to the material?*

- *Have you confirmed that all details will remain confidential?*

- *Do parents have the right to withdraw at any time without explanation – and are they aware of this?*

- *Will parents have access to all the collected information?*

- *Has health and safety been considered?*

The role of the adult as a guardian

The Local Safeguarding Children Board Regulations (2006) were set up as part of the need to protect and promote children's welfare. The concept of 'safeguarding' children aims to protect them from bullying, adverse or unfair discrimination and accidents, and to ensure access to all services. Additionally, the Common Assessment Framework (CAF) intends to protect children in a variety of contexts when there is a concern, as well as when safeguarding issues arise. So, from a legislation perspective, early years professionals have frameworks to work with where observation and assessment are necessary for a child's well-being.

The role of the adult as a guardian is to consider whether or not:

- the observations are in the best interests of the child;
- the observations respect children's privacy, dignity and possible emotional reactions;
- the observations will help the education programme;
- the observations will help to understand the child's development;
- the observations will inform practice and promote children's learning;
- the safety and protection of children is ensured.

Managing the observation recordings in an ethical way

As discussed in earlier chapters, early years practitioners have been using observations to gain both an understanding of children's development and learning, and to inform the planning of activities. Following the introduction of the EYFS – with its pre-set learning outcomes and learning goals – the early years workforce must use formal and structured guidelines, working within a common framework of assessment scales. The EYFS details what information for each child will be gathered through observations in the assessment scales. It also explains the documentation process of observation recordings and offers clear guidelines on how children's profiles should be created. It is stated that records must be kept for *the safe and efficient management of the setting and to meet the needs of the children* (DCSF, 2008a, page 38). The data collected are regulated under the Data Protection Act of 1998 and the Freedom of Information Act of 2000. The EYFS offers guidance on how long records should be kept. It states that *records relating to individual children should be retained for a reasonable period of time (for example, three years) after the children have left provision* (*ibid*, page 40).

Moreover, with the introduction of the CAF, these guidelines are even more structured. The CAF does not aim to replace the everyday observations that take place in the early years setting, but does aim to protect children and prevent any harm.

The CAF has been developed around three steps. The first step is *preparation* to identify if there might be a problem and to decide whether or not to carry out a common assessment; the next step is to carry this out; and the final step is to identify relevant support if working with other services.

The Common Assessment Framework for Children and Young People: A Practitioners' Guide *provides a detailed framework for when children are assessed. Study these guidelines and try to list the ethical implications addressed in them.*

Although there is a wealth of legislation and guidelines, the early years professional has been left feeling that there is an increase in the workload. Brandon *et al.* (2006), in an evaluation of the implementation of the CAF, found that agencies responsible for the CAF did not find it easy to implement a holistic approach to assessment. Working with parents directly and safeguarding parental involvement was a major hurdle. Roles and responsibilities were not always spread across all sectors, as well as not being clear. The conclusion was that the lack of clarity and clear guidance, and the range of skills required, could lead to *anxiety and frustration* among workers and consequently could create conflict and a loss of professional confidence.

With that in mind, the early years professional has been left confused in terms of how he or she can document – and what the purpose of the observation recordings is. Luff (2007) identifies this as a problem in the early years. She claims that observation recording and documentation should have a supportive role in children's learning and in the professional's practice. She argues that documentation should not be just the collection of a number of papers or *a paper exercise duty*, but that it should add value to the educational programme and should be beneficial to the children's assessment.

An important part of the observation process, in addition to the ethical considerations, is the analysis of the observation recordings and how these are kept. However recordings are kept/documented, this should be done in an ethical way. Documentation is part of these ethical concerns.

The remaining question for the early years professional is: how are the observation recordings documented? Where shall the early years professional start? When observation recordings are collected to further our understanding of children's development and learning, as well as to inform practice, then four main questions should be asked:

1. What is the purpose of record keeping?

The purpose should be in line with the aims and objectives of the observation process itself. The purpose is to enable all participants (i.e. the early years team, parents and children) to monitor children's progress and to inform the educational programme. Observation recordings help to ensure continuity of practice in early years settings, which is the ultimate goal of the observation process.

Assessing children's progress and the ability to reflect upon the education programme will help the early years team to cover all the developmental areas suggested by the EYFS, as well as maintaining an understanding of their implementation.

2. What is the use of record keeping?

The observation process is an ongoing and continuous process. The continuous collection of information about a child or a group of children and the educational programme can provide evidence to support assessment and referrals, as requested by the CAF. All this evidence can be used as a communication tool with the parents, as well as with other professionals and authorities, such as Local Education Authorities (LEAs) and Ofsted. Sharing evidence of practice is a helpful way of exploring new pedagogies and experiences.

3. Who are the participants in the process of record keeping?

Those that share an interest in the process are the early years team, the children and the parents, but also the authorities to whom nurseries are accountable.

4. Who has access to the records?

Access to records should be determined by who has a legitimate interest in the process. Access is also determined by the settings' particular regulation, as well as by national legislation. Parents, carers and outside agencies are the ones who will have an interest, as well as the early years team members.

Sharing observations

How these observations and records are shared with parents and/or carers is an important consideration, as accessibility in the observation recording is part of the ethical implications. Drummond says that *paramount among [the early years professional's role and responsibilities] is the responsibility to monitor the effects of their work so as to ensure that their good intentions for children are raised* (1993, page 10).

The Statutory Framework of the EYFS provides clear guidelines on how each child's profile can be created and how information can be shared.

SUMMARY

This chapter raised some issues on ethical implications when observing young children. Within the new policy initiatives, reforms, legislations and curriculum, the early years field has a number of reference points with regard to ethical practices.

However, it is argued in this chapter that ethical implications are not solely about consent, but also concern involvement from all participants in the observation process as well. Observation processes should be underpinned by careful consideration of the ethical issues, and documentation is important to these ethical discussions.

For more on ethical considerations when working with and researching in the early childhood sector:

Palaiologou, I (Ed.) (2012) *Ethical practice in early childhood.* London: SAGE.

For more on ethical issues when researching young children:

Harcourt, D, Perry, B and Waller, T (2011) *Researching Young Children's Perspectives: Debating the ethics and dilemmas of education research with children.* London: Routledge.

Kellet, M (2010) *Rethinking Children and Research: Attitudes in Contemporary Society.* London: Continuum.

For full access to the United Nations Convention on Children's Rights:
United Nations (1989) *The Convention on the Rights of the Child Defense International and the United Nations Children's Fund.* Geneva.

www.unicef.org/crc/

For more on children's voices and examples of children's participation in all aspects of daily life:

www.unicef.org.uk/UNICEFs-Work/Our-mission/Childrens-rights/Voice/

6   Observing for development

Through reading this chapter, you should be able to consider:

- how we observe children's development;
- how we observe children's learning and play;
- the role of the adult in an early years setting.

Observation of young children provides rich information of understanding and extending our knowledge of children's development and learning.

Introduction

In the previous chapters, the role of observation and the methods used, as well as the ethical implications that are an integral part of them, were explored. As discussed previously, observations should become part of the everyday life in the early years setting, being 'woven' into the setting's activities, with children's interactions with other children and with adults. This chapter discusses the role of observations in children's development and learning, with an emphasis on play, and links observations to the EYFS learning goals.

What do we know about children's development?

Chapter 1 offered an overview of theories about children's development, concluding that our early years practice is influenced by theories and by how children are viewed in the social and cultural context. Child development is rooted in moral, social and political choices and problems (Hartley, 1993). These ideas about early childhood result in different approaches to the subject of child development. Understanding why and how children develop in the early years is crucial to professionals, as it influences their approaches to them. Child development is about *anticipation, attainment and assessment* (Robinson, 2008, page 3). The developmental achievements of children are central to early years practice and are important for their progression in life, in order to acquire skills and abilities which they will use for the rest of their lives. Consequently, the ways in which observations are designed are shaped by how we think about children's development.

The Early Years Foundation Stage maintains a *holistic* view of child development and describes the different aspects of this according to four main themes: the healthy child, the competent learner, the skilful communicator and the 'strong' child. While there is an emphasis on this holistic approach, traditionally development is studied in the following separate areas:

- physical and biological development;

- personal, social and emotional development;

- cognitive development;

- language development;

- creativity.

This helps professionals to understand, in a deeper and more effective way, how children develop. However, even though we study development in these separate areas, these often inter-link and impact upon each other.

There is a wealth of literature and research on child development that the early years professional can use to seek guidance and advice. Observation is always the starting point of all developmental theories that seek to expand knowledge and understanding of how children develop. Observation recordings and information are valuable resources and are key to the study of child development. The information collected by different observation techniques provides insights into many aspects of child development.

THEORY FOCUS

Developmental areas and key characteristics

Developmental areas	Key characteristics
Physical development	*Large motor development:* Balancing Walking Running Jumping Climbing *Small motor development:* Hand preference Turns with hand (pages, lids) Holds (pens, pencils, scissors) Dresses and undresses Makes puzzles Builds with small blocks
Emotional development	Shows interest Shows happiness Shows affection Shows enjoyment Shows sympathy Shows empathy Shows distress Shows fear Shows anger Shows sadness

Personal development	Stays in the setting without difficulty
	Makes eye contact
	Develops relationships with early years practitioners
	Makes relationships with other children
	Participates in role play
	Participates in social play
	Participates in symbolic play
	Gets involved in the daily routine of the setting
Social development	*Engaged in:*
	Watching others during play or activities
	Playing by him/herself
	Parallel play
	Play with others
	Making friends
	Having friends
	Following rules
	Taking turns
	Sharing with others
	Seeing things from another point of view
	Helping others during play or activities
Cognitive development	*Attention:*
	Concentration span during activities or play
	Distraction
	Memory:
	Recognises familiar objects and people
	Can name familiar objects and people
	Searches for hidden, favourite objects
	Recalls and narrates stories
	Perception (how sensory information is organised and interpreted):
	Identifying objects, colours
	Locating – is able to know distances, sizes, directions
	Categorising of information into meaningful patterns
	Reasoning
	Problem solving:
	Sorting objects by colour, size, weight
	Classification of objects (big/small, more/less)
	Language:
	Spoken language (uses single words, uses sentences, singing, takes part in conversations, asks questions, narrates a story)

Developmental areas and key characteristics *continued*

Cognitive development	Numeracy: (understands meaning of numbers, understand use of numbers, counting and ordering)
Literacy	Holds a pen/pencil Pretends to write Pretends to read Attempts scribbles Letter-like writing 'Reads' pictures Holds books Turns pages Points at text Narrates stories from the pictures in the book Understands that print conveys messages
Creativity	Makes marks on paper Makes shapes Shows interest in drawing Shows interest in singing Shows interest in dramatic play Shows interest in telling stories/making stories Combines materials and objects together to create e.g. a drawing, story

Table 6.1   Developmental areas and key characteristics

ACTIVITY **1**

Choosing one of the developmental areas, focus on a target child and try to create an observation plan in order to carry out observations to assess this child's development.

First step: find out the age of the child.

Second step: identify what characteristics children have at this age.

Third step: design an observation plan that will help you gain rich evidence of this child's development.

However, because of the limitations of each information gathering technique, many are used in combination to study children and to understand their behaviour. For example, when you look at a child's emotional development, you might want to combine observation techniques such as a checklist, time sampling and narratives. Even in this case, the information collected might not be complete. As a result, it is very important to discuss your findings and concerns with parents, in order to get a better understanding of when and why a certain type of behaviour occurs. You can then draw conclusions about a child's progress in a certain developmental area.

Ben is two years and 16 days old. He has just moved to a village with his mother, father and his older sister. His sister attends the same nursery. Ben's mother provided the nursery with his portfolio from his previous nursery, which Ben attended from the age of nine months. The checklists in his portfolio highlighted Ben's development, with a particular focus on his physical and language development. The nursery staff have already identified that Ben enjoys building, which he will do in the construction area, or the sand or water areas, and whenever he gets the opportunity to build things up high, he will. However, the staff has noticed that he prefers to do this on his own and that he stops when other children join him.

After a team meeting, the staff in the nursery decided to observe Ben to collect further information about him, in order to identify what stage he is at developmentally, and to focus on his social skills, to encourage him to interact more with other children.

They decided to observe him every day for a week. The main focus was social development and the objectives were to observe Ben's interactions with other children during play and activities. They decided to carry out time and event samplings, tracking and narratives. The narratives were in two formats: as participant observations if something occurred and as non-participant observations. The staff in Ben's group shared roles, in order to know when they would observe him. They felt that in this way they could collect the information they needed to effectively assess his social skills. Before beginning, they undertook some further reading on social and emotional development.

Some notes on what we know about social and emotional development:

The early years in a child's life are important for his/her personal, social and emotional development. An environment that is safe, affectionate and encouraging promotes positive feelings in children and develops their social skills. From the moment children are born, they are engaged in interacting with adults in an attempt to become independent and social beings. The early stages of their lives are important for the acquisition of the social and emotional skills that will enhance their personal development.

We tend to study social and emotional development together, as they are interlinked and reinforce each other. Social development has two important aspects. Firstly, children attempt to form an identity and a personality through differentiating themselves as distinctive individuals. Secondly, they try to find a place in the immediate social community and in society at large. From the beginning of life, children try to develop their 'self concept', or an image of themselves: *It is a cognitive construction [. . .] a system of describing and evaluating representations about the self* (Harter, 1996, page 207). The attainment of the concept of self involves the development of a self-image, which is an attempt to understand ourselves and to gain an inner picture of who we are. This acquisition of self-esteem is a process whereby we come to an understanding of our self-worth and value. In the complex process of developing a concept of the self, we are required to achieve appropriate socialisation skills that enable us to interact with our environment. Understanding shared values, beliefs and rules, we make attempts to get to know our social environment and to try to fit into our community.

Emotional development is concerned with our feelings and how we control them in order to respond appropriately on different occasions. Emotions are internal or external reactions to certain situations and will differ from child to child. For example, when children become angry in class, they might express their anger by crying, whereas other children might express anger by becoming sad and withdrawn.

One of the most influential theories about children's emotional development, and one which is very relevant to the early years, is attachment theory, initially developed by Bowlby. Attachment is the bond between the mother or carer and the baby. Secure relationships with the family help children to form positive relationships with others. It is important to understand attachment theory, as children who come to the early years setting at a very young age are asked to separate from their parents or carers and spend time in the early years setting instead. For some children, this experience can be particularly distressing.

It is also important to understand that children's emotional responses have not yet matured and, consequently, they are not able to maintain control over their feelings of distress, anger, sadness, interest, affection or joy. Thus, the early years environment is important in helping children to express their emotions appropriately and, at the same time, in providing opportunities for them to move towards controlling their feelings and expressing them through words.

These are narratives (snapshots) from a participant observation of Ben.

Time	Activity	Social group	Comments
12:00–12:02	Ben sits at the table with two other boys and two girls. The nursery nurse is pouring them all a drink. The children are encouraged to say 'thank you'. Ben says this but sits quietly at the table corner as the other children talk.	2 boys 2 girls	When Ben is encouraged to speak he does. However, he does not feel confident enough to speak to the other children.
12:30–12:32	Ben is washing his hands because they are covered in yogurt. He returns to the table and sits quietly next to a girl.	2 boys 1 girl	Ben shows that he is capable of washing his own hands without help from the staff, but he does not interact with the other children in the bathroom or at the table.

1:00–1:02	The children are singing nursery rhymes and songs. They are sitting on the carpet during the last few minutes of the session. Ben is joining in with singing and arm actions. The nursery nurse has asked the children to pair up so they can sing 'row, row, row your boat' and rock backwards and forwards holding each other's hands. Ben remains sat still on the carpet. The nursery nurse moves Jack over to Ben and partners them up. The two boys hold hands. The singing begins. Ben is not singing but is carrying out the actions. The children are laughing when the nursery rhymes have finished. They sing the nursery rhyme again; Ben joins in and is smiling and laughing at the end.	All children 1 nursery nurse	Ben seems to enjoy the activity. However, he also seems to become uncomfortable when partnered up. When given another opportunity to participate in the nursery rhyme, Ben has relaxed more and joins in with the other children.
1:30–1:32	There are different play-stations set up around the room and staff members are helping children to make a winter picture on the arts table. Ben is playing in the sandpit on his own. He is building a sandcastle.	Solitary play	Ben is choosing to play alone. Other children are playing alongside each other and together on the carpet with cars and trains, but Ben does not join them.
2:00–2:02	Ben is on the carpet in the corner with a box of Duplo bricks and he is building with the yellow pieces. Jack has come over and has also started taking Duplo bricks out of the box. Ben stops playing. After 30 seconds Jack hands Ben a yellow piece that he has pulled out of the box. *Oh look, yellow*, he says. *Thanks*, Ben replies, taking the piece. He looks at Jack and he picks up two more pieces.	Solitary play, and then parallel play with Jack	Ben still seems wary of what other children are doing, but perhaps this is because it is only his second week in this group. It is positive to see that Ben is able to play alongside Jack with the same toys.
2:30–2:32	The nursery nurse calls Ben and Jack over to make their Christmas pictures. Ben is talking to the nursery nurses quite confidently and, when asked which colours he wants on his picture, he keeps saying the same colours as Jack wants to use.	Jack Nursery nurse	Ben appears to listen to what Jack says and he repeats the same colours. It might be an attempt to 'share' with Jack.

3:00–3:02	*Ben is playing in the sand area on his own again. Jack is also present. A girl has begun to play at the opposite side of the sand tray. Jack continues to play with his bucket and spade. Where have all the spades gone?* she asks. Jack bends underneath the tray and passes a spade to the girl.	Sand area Ben and Jack	Ben plays alongside with Jack, yet he does not seem to be interacting or sharing with him, but he stays there even when another child arrives to play.
3:30–3:32	The children are sat all together on the carpet listening to the nursery nurse reading from a 'big book'. Ben is sat next to Jack and he pays attention to the story.	All children in the room with the nursery nurse	Although Ben is listening to the story, he has chosen to sit next to Jack.
4:00–4:02	Ben is asleep on large beanbags.		Ben is usually picked up at 3:30 but his mother said she would be late, so the nursery staff has let him sleep.
4:30–4:32	Ben is woken up by his mother and he smiles when he sees her. His mother puts his jacket on, collects his bag and carries him out of the room. Ben turns his head and says, *Bye, Jack.* He raises his left hand to wave 'goodbye' to Jack.	Mother Nursery nurse Jack	Ben has shown a positive sign by waving to Jack. It seems that he is starting to like Jack and is showing an interest in socialising with him.

Table 6.2 Narratives from a participant observation

Ben's behaviour is analysed during a halfday when he is in class.

Behaviours	Carpet area	Construction area	Water tray	Role play area	Sand tray
Ben talks to another child.	**	****	**	******	*
Ben does not talk to another child.	*********	***********	**********	*************	*************
Ben plays alongside another child.	*************	****************	**********	************	*****************
Ben leaves when another child arrives.	**	**********	**********	******	****

Table 6.3 Example of event sampling technique

By collecting a number of observation recordings (above are only two of a variety of examples carried out within the space of a week), staff analysed the information. They concluded that Ben is making progress in terms of interacting with others and that he has started settling into the new setting and making positive progress in his social development. It appears from the observation recordings that it may take a while longer before he becomes completely relaxed and confident with his new situation, but he will eventually become more familiar with the new routine. The staff looked at developmental stages and they concluded that Ben plays in parallel with other children but that he has not yet moved to play co-operatively. They decided to discuss all the observation findings with his parents and to ask them their opinion.

What do we know about children's learning?

The early years learning environment is dominated by a play-orientated pedagogy. A number of studies (Moyles, *et al.*, 2001; Sylva *et al.*, 2001; Siraj-Blatchford and Sylva, 2002; Taylor with Aubrey *et al.*, 2002) found that children's learning is enhanced in settings where there is a balance between both adult- and child-initiated activities. Learning is also enhanced where practice is planned within a framework of observation and assessment, with parental involvement, and by liaising with other services.

In Chapter 1 it was discussed that, in order to create a learning environment for children, some conditions of learning need to be taken into consideration. These are the emphasis on:

- children's development;

- play;

- children's needs;

- children's freedom to choose materials and activities;

- children's ownership of their own learning.

However, these conditions are not directly linked to children's learning alone. The role of the adult is also important, as learning will not occur in an environment where these conditions exist without the support of adults. As discussed in Chapter 1 under the cognitive psychology theory, the interactions with the environment (Piagetian approach) and the role of adult as a more experienced peer (Vygotskian idea of ZPD) are central in educational settings where children develop their physical, emotional, social and cognitive skills such as linguistic concepts, lexis, language, problem solving and mathematical concepts. Children's early experiences can be enhanced by interaction with adults during their play.

Play underpins early years practice. It is suggested that adults hold a key role in assisting children's play both indoors and outdoors. It is recognised in the EYFS that children through play: *investigate and experience things, and 'have a go'* (DfE, 2012a, page 7).

Through play, children acquire skills within a given context. A number of studies on play and learning (Athey, 1990; Nutbrown, 1999) suggest that children are able to develop planned and purposeful play, and the role of the adult is to base the planning for the educational programme on this. These studies point out that learning through play can be put at risk in a framework where learning outcomes are target driven. As mentioned in Chapter 1, play for a young child is spontaneous and lacks organisation. Consequently learning through play can become unpredictable, as children's interests or needs may take unplanned and unforeseen directions. These, however, are valid learning opportunities for children, as they build upon their own interests and needs, and as they take ownership of their own play and learning. The role of the adult is crucial in an environment that values play as enabling children to be creative. Professionals' support, intervention, interaction and planning can assist children's play and can enable them to benefit from that play.

In a play-based learning environment, observations are equally important and integral to constantly monitoring children's progress. Observations can become a valuable tool to collect information in context and to ensure that the assessment of children will be meaningful. Such assessments will demonstrate not only what children can do and what different skills they have acquired, but also how they use those skills.

Working within a framework such as the Early Years Foundation Stage has some constraints, as intended learning outcomes are not always realistically observable and measurable, nor are they easily achieved by children. Observing children's learning for assessment purposes in an environment with set learning goals requires:

- communication with parents, in order to set appropriate expectations from both sides, and to involve parents in the observation process;
- space and resources applicable to the adult/child ratio;
- built-in time for effective team meetings and the preparation of the observations' design;
- the development of effective observation systems and record keeping;
- training.

CASE STUDY

Louise is two years and eight months. She attends nursery three times per week. In the following observation, the tracking technique has been used. It not only demonstrates Louise's preferences during play, but also how she uses her social skills during it:

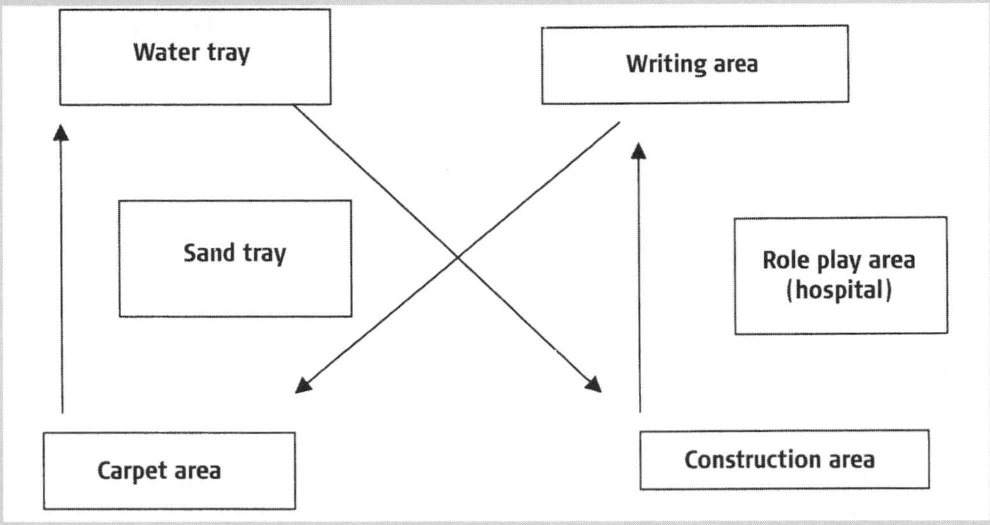

Figure 6.1 Louise's preferences of play areas

Start: 2:10pm (15 minutes in carpet area)
Sat on the carpet with a friend. Louise is showing her friend photographs and narrates what she was doing when these photographs were taken (from her summer holidays).

2:25 (8 minutes, water tray area)
Louise and her friend move to the water area and they are sorting out different shells into groups. Louise's friend leaves her and goes to the sand tray. After two minutes, Louise also leaves but she does not follow her friend.

2:33 (13 minutes in the construction area)
Louise plays on her own and she creates a strong, well-built model using magnetic blocks.

2:46 (14 minutes in the writing area)
Louise sits at a table with two other children. She has chosen to colour in a picture of a 'Gruffalo'. She is doing this with care, and at the same time she talks to other children.

Finish: 3:00 Children are called to the carpet area and Louise goes there with her picture.

The role of the adult

Working with children in the early years requires a number of skills, such as a good understanding and theoretical knowledge of child development, a good understanding of children's abilities and how they learn from play, an understanding of effective pedagogy and administrative skills. Among these skills, the early years workforce needs very good observation, as the observation recordings offer insights into children's development and learning and enable the professional to create appropriate learning environments within the curriculum.

It is vital for the early years workforce to understand the theoretical underpinnings of its own practice. The view of the child as a confident learner, able to choose his or her materials and activities, will determine the observation process. Children's development and what they are able to do at a given stage of their lives then needs to be looked at. This knowledge may result from literature on general aspects of development, but also from direct observations of children themselves. Knowing the individual children in your group, and their abilities, interests and needs, is the starting point for planning new activities and experiences. The main tools of validation are observations of children, taking into account both parental and child involvement. The observation recording will then be interpreted and become important information for assessing early years practice. These findings are an important tool to share with parents and children, in order to encourage and enable the children's participation in classroom life.

SUMMARY

This chapter discussed observations in relation to children's development and learning. Observations offer us information and evidence for understanding and extending our knowledge of their development and learning. Observing for development and learning through play has some constraints, as it requires time and a high level of skill from the professional. However, it is a valid tool as it informs everyday practice with children.

Working within the Early Years Foundation Stage, there is a clear emphasis on observation and assessment for children, for formative and summative purposes. Within this framework, the early years workforce has to demonstrate skills and effective practice in observation and to lead and support the development of observation skills in others. The role is challenging in the context of new policies and the implementation of the EYFS.

FURTHER READING

For more on children's development;

Dowling, M (2005) *Young Children's Personal and Social Development.* (2nd ed.). London: Paul Chapman.

Nutbrown, C (2007) *Threads of thinking* (2nd ed.). London: Paul Chapman.

Penn, H (2005) *Understanding Early Childhood: Issues and Controversies.* Maidenhead: Open University Press.

Robinson, M (2008) *Child Development from Birth to Eight: A Journey Through the Early Years.* Maidenhead: Open University Press.

For more information on observing development:

Beaty, J (2006) *Observing for Development in Young Children* (6th ed.). New Jersey: Pearson Merrill Prentice Hall.

For more on planning and observation:

Bradford, H (2012) *Planning and observation of children under three.* London: David Futon Book.

Hobart, C and Frankel, J (2004) *A Practical Guide to Child Observations and Assessments* (3rd ed.). Cheltenham: Stanley Thornes.

7   Observing for research

Through reading this chapter, you will:

- consider observation as a research method;

- consider the differences between observation as a research method and observation as part of your practice;

- be aware that observation is a method that produces qualitative as well as quantitative data;

- understand how to record and analyse observation for research purposes.

There is a difference when you use observations for practice and when you use observations for research. Observing for research purposes should provide valid and rigorous data.

Introduction: origins of observation

Throughout this book, we have explored the role of observation in early years settings and practice. Observations in the field of education are widely used and they are part of the everyday routine of the classroom as a way of gaining an in-depth understanding of children's development and learning in order to reflect to the educational activities of the classroom. However, observation has been used in research from many fields of study as an in-depth investigation of a single person, group, event or community. In the field of early childhood studies, pioneers such as Montessori or Isaacs introduced observations from their own fields.

For example, Montessori had studied medicine and she was involved in early childhood education originally as a doctor for children with disabilities and it was then when she developed an interest in the education of young children. Her method of systematic observation was heavily influenced by her disciplined training in medicine.

Another example is Susan Isaacs, who brought psycho-analytical ideas to the education of young children. Influenced by the psycho-analytical work of Anna Freud and Melanie Klein, she was the first to bring in these ideas and to modify them to the needs of an educational setting. Under Melanie Klein's influence and through systematic observations, she demonstrated that play was not only about children's mastery of the world and learning but also an equally important means of expression and emotional relief.

Observation is widely used in social sciences as a research method to collect data. As discussed in Chapter 2, observation in a nursery setting is an activity that involves systematic watching of others in their natural environment such as customs, beliefs and way of life.

In Chapter 1, when considering the different psychological theories, the pioneering work of Erick Bick (1964) in the field of psycho-analytical infant observation was cited as a useful research tool to understand the interactions between mothers and their babies. This work was extended by the work of Bowlby. The field of cognitive psychology took observation of young children to another level with the Piagetian tests and the systematic measurements of certain behaviours that occurred when the tests were carried out. Of course observation is not only used by the social sciences but by other sciences such as medicine, astronomy, the physical sciences, biology and so on.

The most dominant observation methods are summarised in the following theory focus box:

THEORY FOCUS

Observation as a research tool

Method	Description	Nature	Tools	Strengths	Limitations	Examples
Naturalistic observation	Observation of behaviour in its natural context. The researcher pretends that he/she is part of the group being observed.	Natural Unstructured Participant	Written observations (narratives). Digital media to record mainly field notes (narrative, qualitative data) searching for meaning in the text.	Observation Reflects participants' everyday lives, habits, customs, values.	Conditions under which participants are observed cannot be controlled.	Psycho-analytical infant observation. Bowlby's observations on attachment.
Structured observation	Observation of a behaviour in a laboratory or in a controlled context. Observer has no contact with the participants.	Controlled Structured Non-participant	Brief written observations. Rating scales. Checklists. Diagrammatic (mainly quantitative data, searching for meaning through a numerical approach).	Conditions of observation are the same for all participants so a certain behaviour can be measured/recorded.	Observation may not be typical of the participants' behaviour in everyday life.	Bandura's experiments on observational learning: Bobodoll. Behaviourists' experiments of conditioning Piagetian tests of children's cognitive development.

Self-observation	Observation of self-behaviour in a variety of contexts as a way of investigating these behaviours.	Purpose-specific	Digital media, diaries, journals (mainly narrative, qualitative data, searching for meaning through text).	Self-observation offers an in-depth understanding of internal or external behaviours which caused certain actions/reactions.	Observations are subjective and can be skewed by the researcher's personal beliefs and values.	Self-observation is used widely in treatments for recovery (alcohol, drugs). As a student, you use self-observation when doing reflective portfolios. Early years practitioners use self-observation for reflection.

Table 7.1   Observation as a research tool

Observation and research

Planning a research project can be an adventurous process. Sometimes it is fascinating and at other times difficulties must be overcome. Maykut and Morehouse point out the significant role planning plays in a research project:

The questions we ask will always to some degree determine the answers we find. This point is important in designing a qualitative study. The research questions that guide a qualitative study reflect the researcher's goal of discovering what is important to know about some topic of interest. A qualitative study has a focus but that focus is initially broad and open-ended, allowing for important meanings to be discovered.

(1994, page 26)

Experienced researchers agree that undertaking a research project can have unknown elements. Even though there are numerous papers and books in the literature to help a researcher, the field can nevertheless be *messy*, *frustrating* and *unpredictable* (Wellington, 1996, page 7). Even so, a review of existing literature on methodology is helpful in order to design the appropriate methodology on which to build the theoretical background for any study you wish to undertake.

In order to decide appropriate observation methods to investigate your research questions, it is necessary to establish the kind of data required and to explore your research objectives. Two important issues must be taken into account when observation methods are used with children. In the first place, it is important to decide how to measure the progress they make throughout the observation process. Secondly, there is a need to choose observation methods that will enable data to be collected in order to gain an in-depth understanding of what you are investigating.

As can be seen in the theory focus box above, observation can be a method for qualitative as well as quantitative research. The following sections aim to discuss these two methodological traditions and how they can be combined.

Observation as a qualitative method

Maykut and Morehouse (1994) point out that a qualitative approach offers the researcher the opportunity to go in depth and discover *important meanings* when conducting the studies. Qualitative observation helps the researcher to understand important meanings and gain insights into an under-researched field. However, this method is not as useful for measuring children's progress but quantitative observation will provide the measurement tools in these circumstances.

Much of the discussion in the literature about these two approaches has created a somewhat exaggerated picture of their differences. These discussions tend to treat quantitative and qualitative research as though they are naturally antagonistic, ideal types of research processes. This tendency can be clearly discerned in some of the statements relating to qualitative research. However, while there are differences between the two research methods, there are also a number of points at which the differences are not as rigid as the statements often imply. Consequently, in addressing some of the features of quantitative and qualitative research, some areas of similarity will also be identified. At this point, it will be helpful to broaden the discussion and investigate how combining qualitative and quantitative observation as methods can provide the full range of data required.

In order to do this, we first need to investigate the role of the two research methods and then investigate the problems that may result when they are combined. It is also essential to examine how the data from these two methods can be linked in order to offer the possibility of reliable and valid conclusions.

As outlined earlier, qualitative research tends to be concerned with words rather than numbers in order to offer an *in-depth* investigation. Bryman (2004), Bryman and Burgess (1999) and Silverman (2011) identify three main features of qualitative research.

First, they suggest that there is a relationship between theory and research. There are two main trends. The practitioners of grounded theory claim that the importance of qualitative research relies on the fact that it allows theoretical ideas to emerge out of the researcher's data (Strauss, 1967; Charmaz, 2000). Some qualitative researchers argue that qualitative data can perform an important role in relation to the testing of theories. Silverman (2011) claims that more recently, qualitative research has become increasingly interested in the testing of theories, a reflection of the growing maturity of the strategy. The data should offer evidence to test the theory that underpins the research in order to establish whether it can provide an alternative for future educational programmes and practice.

Second, qualitative research is informed by an epistemological position, which is described as interpretivist (Bryman, 2004; Gubrium and Holstein, 1997). The emphasis of qualitative research is on understanding the social world through an examination of the interpretation of that world by its participants. Finally, there is an ontological view that the social phenomena researched are not separated from those involved in its construction. The epistemological and ontological views of the qualitative research reflect on its nature. Qualitative research is not a straightforward strategy (Bryman and Burgess, 1999) but rather a complex strategy and therefore it is difficult to specify its nature.

Even though researchers, such as Silverman (2011), argue that it is difficult to identify the nature of qualitative research, Gubrium and Holstein (1997) suggest four traditions.

THEORY FOCUS

Four key traditions in qualitative research

Tradition	Characteristics
Naturalistic tradition	Seeks to understand social reality and provide a full account of descriptions of people and interactions in natural settings
Ethnomethodological tradition	Seeks to understand how social order is created through talk and interaction
Emotionalist tradition	Seeks to understand the inner reality of humans and exhibits a concern with subjectivity and gaining access to inside experience
Post-modern tradition	Seeks ways to emphasise the different ways in which social reality can be constructed.

Table 7.2   Traditions in qualitative research

There are two reasons why it is essential to identify the nature of qualitative research and existing traditions. In the first place, qualitative research includes several diverse methods that are quite different from each other. Thus, it is essential that the nature of the qualitative research you aim to apply to your study is identified, in order to choose the most appropriate method for producing the required data and for investigating how theory can be tested in a social context.

The second reason for the importance of identifying the nature of qualitative research is the connection between the theory, the research forms and the collection and analysis of the data. Your study should aim to investigate how theory can be translated into activities in order to facilitate children's development and learning. The findings will feed back into the relevant theory.

Observation as a quantitative method

Quantitative research, in very broad terms, is described as entailing the collection of numerical data and investigating the relationship between these and the theory. Quantitative research uses a special language – variable, control, measurements, experiment – in order to analyse the data and a distinctive epistemology and ontology.

The epistemological and ontological views suggest that quantitative research moves beyond the mere presence of numbers and that the epistemology upon which quantitative research *is erected comprises a litany of pre-conditions for what is warrantable knowledge* (Bryman, 1992, page 12).

It often has a logical structure in which theories determine the problems which researchers address (Bryman, 2004). It is commonly used to examine patterns of interactions such as studies of teacher child, early years workforce, children interaction. Surveys and experiments are the most common methodological tools of quantitative research, but structured observations and content analysis are two others. (Beardsworth, 1980; Keat and Urry, 1975).

The different nature of these two research methods reflects the differences in the main features of qualitative and quantitative research. Bryman (2001, 2004) identifies some main differences between these two methods, related to the dimensions on which these diverge. These differences are related to the structure, design purposes and nature of the data of the two methods. Smith takes the argument further and claims that each of the two research strategies *sponsors different procedures and has different epistemological implications* (1983, pages 12–13) and therefore researchers should not *accept the unfounded assumption that the methods are complementary*. These two research strategies are oriented by distant epistemological and ontological commitments (Hughes, 1990) and thus, qualitative inquiry should be separated from quantitative inquiry (Smith and Heshusius, 1986).

Guba (1985) and Morgan (1998) agree with the above and add *the paradigm* argument in this debate. They suggest that quantitative and qualitative research as paradigms differ in terms of epistemological assumptions, values and methods. Therefore, these paradigms are incommensurable (Kuhn, 1970) and there are no areas of overlap and commonality between them (Hughes, 1990; Walker, 1985; Rist, 1977). However, it is argued in the following section that, depending on the nature of the research question, there are times when these two different research methods can be combined and harmonised to facilitate the collection of appropriately rich data.

ACTIVITY **1**

Study the theory focus box. Can you identify which observation methods are qualitative and which are quantitative and why?

Combining qualitative and quantitative observation methods

In the above section, the nature of qualitative and quantitative research methods was examined and it was shown that they differ in terms of epistemology, ontology, paradigm, organisation and data analysis (see theory focus box below). In combining these two different research methods and the two kinds of argument thus stimulated, it was necessary to examine the epistemological and ontological commitments that these methods involve and also the paradigm argument that reflects the organisation of the research design and the data analysis. In addition, the issue of how the data will be linked should also be considered. In the following paragraphs therefore, an attempt is made to discuss these difficulties in order to overcome any problems which might influence the reliability, validity and generalisation of the findings.

THEORY FOCUS

Research

Research is:

The systematic, controlled, empirical and critical investigation of hypothetical propositions about behaviours, phenomena, relationships and their interactions in a natural or controlled environment (Kerlinger, 1970).

Seeking through methodological processes to add to one's body of knowledge and, hopefully to that of others, by discovering non-trivial facts and insights (Howard and Sharp, 1983, page 6).

A search or investigation directed to the discovery of some facts by careful consideration or study of a subject; a course of critical or scientific inquiry (OED, 2011).

A systematic enquiry made public (Stenhouse, 1975).

A systematic, critical and self-critical inquiry which aims to contribute to the advancement of knowledge (Bassey, 1990, page 35).

Research requires:

- the collection of quite large amounts of data;

- results which can be generalised;

- a hypothesis to be tested or a research question;

- the undertaking of experiments or the use of statistics;

- objectivity rather than subjectivity or subjective reality;

- that something is proved or strongly indicated;

- specific expertise.

Key terms in research:
Ontology: The nature of reality.
Epistemology: The relationship between the researcher and the known world.
Axiology: The researcher's values base.
Rhetoric: The language of research.
Methodology: The process of research.
Paradigm: The way of understanding the world and the human behaviour within it.

Key actions in research:

- establishing the research question(s);

- exploring research options and designing a research project;

- identifying the limits of your study; delimiting appropriately;

- recognising the potential for bias;

- determining a realistic time line for data collection, analysis, interpretation and reporting.

While a great body of social researchers argue against the combination of quantitative and qualitative research due to their different natures, (Hughes, 1990; Smith, 1983; Smith and Heshusius; 1986; Kuhn, 1970) a large number of others appear to be in favour of combining them or, as they claim, using multi-strategy research or mixed method studies (Bryman, 2001, 2004; Hammersley, 1996; Webb *et al.*, 1996; Deacon *et al.*, 1998; Denzin, 1970; Layder, 1993; Tashakkori and Teddlie, 1998).

To begin with the paradigm argument, it is claimed that quantitative and qualitative research methods cannot be compatible. According to these theorists (Smith, 1983; Guba, 1987; Lincoln, 1990, 1994), researchers who try to combine the two methods are likely to fail due to the inherent differences in the paradigm underlying them. However, the opposing view is that the differences between the two paradigms have been *overdrawn* and *the schism* is not as wide as has been portrayed (Tashakkori and Teddlie, 1998). House (1994), in an attempt to explain this *dichotomisation*, claims that it is a result of the *misunderstanding of science*. It was believed that there was either one way or another and that there was *no guaranteed methodological path to the promised land* (House, 1994, pages 20–21).

Smith, though, has a strong argument about the incompatibility of the paradigms of these two methods:

> *One approach takes a subject-object position on the relationship to the subject matter; the other takes a subject-subject position. One separates facts and values, while the other sees them as inextricably mixed. One searches for laws, and the other seeks understanding. These positions do not seem compatible.*

> (1983, page 12)

Therefore, compatibility between qualitative and quantitative research seems impossible due to the incompatibility of paradigms that underlie the methods.

However, Datta (1994) provides arguments against Smith's idea of incompatibility and tries to justify the *coexistence* between the two methodologies and their underlying paradigms. He claims that all the paradigms have been used for many years and that many evaluators and researchers have therefore supported the use of both. A number of researchers have supported both and both paradigms have influenced policy and practice. Last, but not least, both paradigms can contribute and have contributed to knowledge.

Howe (1988) defends this orientation by calling the incompatibility of the two paradigms a *pseudo-problem* and suggests that researchers could use both of them in their research. He argues that research philosophy should move away from the discussion of concepts and become *deconstructive* (page 15). Brewer and Hunter, in an attempt to justify the compatibility of the two paradigms, made a similar point and claimed that *rather than being wed to a particular theoretical style ... and its most compatible method, one might instead combine methods that would encourage or even require integration of different theoretical perspectives to interpret data* (1989, page 74).

Thus, it can be argued that combining two different paradigms can actually work in favour of the research because the use of mixed methods helps the researcher gain a range of information that would not be provided by the restrictive use of one or other of the methods. Moreover, the data can be interpreted and explained under many theories in order to provide significant results and thus the importance of *communicating results* from different paradigms helps the researchers to overcome the fact that the *world is complex and stratified and often difficult to understand* (Reichart and Rallis, 1994, page 84).

However, while combining quantitative and qualitative research might offer a rich data source, the actual methods of collecting these data have certain epistemological and ontological limitations that should be acknowledged. Platt (1996) claims that the notion that research methods reflect or reveal certain assumptions about knowledge and social reality has to be questioned. When the use of research methods in practice is examined, the connections are not absolute. The results of using a method associated with one research strategy should be cross-checked against the results of using the research method of another (Fielding and Fielding, 1986). The traditional quantitative approach to data collection involves relatively detailed and planned tools (Tashakkori and Teddlie, 1998). On the other hand, the most traditional qualitative research has been conducted without such pre-planned methods of data collection.

Miles and Huberman illustrate this problem thus:

> *Knowing what you want to find out, at least initially, leads inexorably to the question of how you will gather information ... some technical choices must be made. Will notes be taken? Of what sort? Will the transaction be tape recorded? Listened to afterwards? Transcribed? How will notes be written up?*
>
> (1994, page 35)

In essence, there is a data collection problem when quantitative and qualitative methods are combined which can influence the way the data will be linked when analysed. Even though a mixed method data collection approach offers an advantage for using both strategies, it can be a limitation at the same time. Amstrong *et al.* (1997) support this limitation and suggest that *reliability* and *validity* are fundamental concerns when combining quantitative and qualitative research. Thus it is important to define these two terms.

Reliability refers to the consistency or repeatability of measures of behaviour. Reliable observations of people's actions are not unique to a single observer (Tedlock, 2000). Instead, observers must agree on what they see and, in this study, the aim is for all the outcomes of observations to be discussed with the teachers who will be directly involved and also with the parents who will be indirectly involved.

Validity is the extent to which measures in a research study accurately reflect what the investigator intends to measure, so reliability is essential for valid research. Due to the difficulties associated with validity, Denzin (1970) describes two types of validity in observationally based studies:

1. External validity considers factors that ensure that the results are applicable to other situations, and;
2. Internal validity considers factors that ensure that the results are the genuine product.

When mixed methods are used, researchers should check and cross-check data from combining methodologies.

Generalisation

A problem arising from the combination of quantitative and qualitative methods is generalisation. Qualitative research often relies on illustrative anecdotal methods of presenting data and thus *the critical reader is forced to ponder whether the researcher has selected only those fragments of data which support his argument* (Silverman, 1985, page 40). Quantitative research also cannot generalise its findings beyond the confines of the particular context in which the research was conducted (Bryman, 2001). However, one question on which a great deal of discussion has centred concerns external validity. It is essential to appreciate that there is a certain limitation to generalisation and that this applies to the present research.

So far, there has been an attempt to discuss some of the issues that arise when quantitative and qualitative research are combined, as in this study. There have been references to the limitations that occur through the incompatibility of quantitative and qualitative research in respect of the reliability, validity and generalisation of the findings. Thus it is essential to develop a research design that will allow the gathering of data and, at the same time, minimise the acknowledged limitations. The following section presents the research design and the methodological tools for data collection and discusses the above limitations.

Observation as a research method versus observation as practice

It is important to distinguish between observation as a tool for informing practice and collecting evidence to understand children's development and learning in your early years setting and observation as a research tool. Throughout this book, we are dealing with observation in relation to early years practice. The key difference using observation as a research tool is the generation of an intensive, detailed examination of the phenomenon or behaviour under study. The observations used as a research method are a reflection of the research inquiry in order to provide a complete collection of data that will enable the researcher to answer the research questions. The findings can be generalised.

Observation as a tool to gain evidence of your practice or children's development and learning is a systematic way of collecting a wealth of information about individual children or group of children or activities in your early years setting over a period of time. However, the findings are indicative and they cannot necessarily be generalised and applied in another setting.

CASE STUDY

Observation as a research tool
(an example of physical development)

Although there is a plethora of literature and research about children's physical development, you want to investigate the physical development of young babies.

You are interested in investigating what physical attributes babies of the age 6–12 months have.

Research design

As part of this research project and in order to collect in-depth evidence, you have developed a research design that involves the combination of qualitative and quantitative observation methods. Your observation schedule contains:

1. Naturalistic observations of young babies in their families and settings using digital media. To complete these, you will analyse the videos in order to categorise what physical skills you have observed in the babies.

2. Structured observation: use of rating scales.

You aim to apply some specific observations in order to identify certain physical attributes.
Babies 6–7 months: give babies blocks of Lego and record and rate their reactions.
Babies 7–9 months: give blocks of Lego and record and rate their reactions.

Repeat the same observation for about five to six times on each of these babies. Findings from each observation will be correlated in one rating scale for each child. The two rating scales will be concluded, one for the group of 6–7 month-old babies and one for the group 7–9 month-old babies. The two rating scales will enable comparisons to be made between the children's performances.

As can be seen, tools from two different methods are employed to provide data for this study. Qualitative observations will be made in order to provide data on children's physical attributes and quantitative methods will facilitate the comparison between the two age groups as a way of measuring progress in their physical development. The findings may offer insights into infants' physical development and with what objects they are interacting physically.

Observation as part of your practice

You work with babies (6–12 months) in a day nursery. You want to collect evidence to assenss children's physical development. In order to collect evidence you have developed the following checklist:

Physical development	attempting	yes	no
Has little or no lag when pulled up to sit			
Can lift head and shoulders when lying on front			
Sits with back straight when supported			
Can hold head steady when upright			
When helped standing, takes weight on feet and bounces			
up and down can roll from front to back			
Can roll from back to front			
Can sit without support			
While sitting can reach forward for a toy without falling over			
Moves around slowly by crawling or bottom shuffling			
Can pull self to standing position			
Can get from a lying to a sitting position			
Walks around a room holding on to furniture			
Stands alone			
Walks with adult help			
Crawls up stairs			
Walks a few steps alone			
Walks across the room when held by one hand			
Walks pushing large wheeled toys			
Can climb on to a low chair and sit down			

Activity:

From which items in the Physical Development: Moving and Handling of the Development Matters in the EYFS (page 22) will you be able to collect information?

• What items would you have deleted?

• What items would you have included?

In the above examples, try to identity a list of the similarities and differences when observation is used for research and when observation is used in early years practice.

SUMMARY

This chapter aimed to discuss observation as a research method highlighting the difference between observation for research and observation for practice. There are differences between these two types. The main one is that when observation is used for research the findings need to be valid, reliable and generalisable.

FURTHER READING

For more on observation as a method for research:

Gillham, B (2008) *Observation techniques: Structured to Unstructured.* London: Continuum.

Chapter 6: *Observation* in Plowright, D (2011*) Using Mixed Methods: Frameworks for an Integrated Methodology.* London: SAGE.

For more on interpreting observation data, read Chapter 5 of:

Silverman, D (2011) *Interpreting Qualitative Data* (4th ed.). London: SAGE.

For more on the difference between observation as a research method and observation as part of practice, read Chapter 12 of:

Papatheodorou, T, Luff, P and Gill, J (2011) *Child observation for learning and research.* Harlow: Pearson.

8   Observing for the curriculum

Through reading this chapter, you will further your understanding of:

- contemporary approaches to pedagogy;

- approaches to the curriculum;

- the differences between pedagogy and curriculum;

- keys ideas on a curriculum for early years;

- the role of observation in the early years curriculum.

Observation planning is an essential activity in early years as it enhances practice and offers meaningful links between children's learning and development and the early years curriculum.

Introduction: Towards an understanding of pedagogy and curriculum

In Chapter 1 we discussed the factors that influence pedagogy in early years. We discussed the social constructions of childhood and the philosophical thinking and psychological thinking that influence pedagogy. In this chapter we will return to the discussion of pedagogy in order to address the differences between pedagogy and curriculum and identify key issues in observing for the curriculum.

As mentioned in Chapter 1, pedagogy is a term that aims to describe a body of knowledge which is concerned with teaching and practice in learning environments. The discussion about the nature of pedagogy is an ongoing one which will never be finalised. Indeed, the more we examine the concept of pedagogy, the more we further our understanding. Contemporary views of pedagogy, mainly influenced by the views of Bruner, introduce the idea of *meta-cognitive pedagogy* (Bruner, 1996). In their view, pedagogy is concerned with the child and to what extent the child is aware of her/his own thought processes when learning and thinking.

Another body of theorists introduced the idea of *critical pedagogy* (Giroux, 2011; Hall 2007; Mohanty, 1989) with an emphasis on how knowledge is used in a responsible and critical way to raise questions about the world in which children live. They believe that constant critical questioning, based on knowledge gained, is a powerful tool to change and improve the world.

Critical pedagogy asserts that students engage their own learning from a position of agency and in so doing can actively participate in narrating identities through a culture of questioning that opens up a space of translation between the private and the public while engaging the forms of self and social recognition.

(Giroux, 2011, page 14)

Papatheodorou and Moyles (2009) suggest that pedagogy should be understood within the *relationality* between *the infinite attention which we owe to each other* (2009, page 5). They describe pedagogy as a form of dialogue between teachers and learners in social and cultural contexts. In an earlier study, Brownlee (2004) defined relational pedagogy in terms of three key elements that characterise the relationship of the learner with the teacher and the learning environment. It is claimed that relational pedagogy is concerned with the respect between the knower and the teacher, the relation between knowledge and the learner's own experiences and finally with the construction of knowledge as a way of acquiring meaning making rather than an accumulation of knowledge. Moyles *et al.* thought that relational pedagogy:

[. . .] connects the relatively self-contained act of teaching and being an early years educator, with personal cultural and community values (including care), curriculum structures and external influences. Pedagogy in the early years operates from a shared frame of reference (a mutual learning encounter) between the practitioner, the young children and his/her family.

(2002, page 5)

Finally Taguchi (2010) suggests a new approach to pedagogy – *intra-active pedagogy* – where it is concerned with the engagement of learners, the value of previous experiences and activities and with the construction of knowledge as a tool for making meaning. Intra-active pedagogy shifts the attention from the traditional ways of creating a learning environment to intra-active relationships between the learners and the use of their immediate environments in their everyday life such as artefacts, spaces and places.

The discussion about pedagogy is a lengthy one and mainly abstract and theoretical, so Barad draws our attention to the fact that:

to theorise is not to leave the material world behind and enter the domain of pure ideas where the lofty space of the mind makes objective reflections possible. Theorising, like experimenting, is a materials process . . . [they are] dynamic practices of materials engagements with the world.

(2007, page 54)

Creating learning environments is about developing an in-depth understanding of what pedagogy is in order to formulate a curriculum that underpins and reflects our views of pedagogy. Consequently, a key distinction between pedagogy and curriculum is that pedagogy is the theoretical approach that will be implemented via the curriculum. Before we discuss the differences between pedagogy and curriculum it is important to try to define the 'curriculum'.

What is curriculum?

Like the discussion about pedagogy, a number of theorists have expressed different views and approaches to the curriculum. Schiro (2008) examined ideological approaches and proposed four dominant approaches:

- the scholar-academic ideology;

- the social efficiency ideology;

- the learner-centred ideology;

- the socio-reconstruction ideology.

The scholar-academic ideology approach is based on the view that knowledge is organised into academic disciplines. Thus, the curriculum is organised around the academic disciplines and the learners are direct subjects who reflect these academic disciplines.

The social efficiency approach views the curriculum as part of the training required to meet the needs of society. It is heavily influenced by behaviourist psychology which promotes the view that learning is a change in a human's behaviour and as such the focus of such a curriculum approach is the concept of learning and the organisation of learning environments and experiences to lead to desired responses by and the accountability of learners.

Learner-centred ideology extends this view: it promotes the idea that learning contains the needs of the society and the academic disciplines, but based on the needs of individual learners. This ideology views the curriculum as an enjoyable experience for the learner, where the learner's cognitive, social, emotional and physical attributes are helped to develop. Learner-centred curricula place emphasis on organisation of the environments where learners are seeking meaning by constant interactions with others and materials.

Finally, *the socio-reconstruction ideology* approach is concerned with the problems of society. Within this approach, curriculum is a social process and should be organised in a way that helps learners to understand their society and contribute to its improvement.

In an earlier study, Marsh examined a number of curricular approaches in education. He categorised these according to the emphasis of their organisation and their aims and objectives:

- curriculum is such *permanent* subjects as grammar, reading, logic, rhetoric, mathematics and the greatest books of the western world that best embody essential knowledge;

- curriculum is those subjects that are most useful for living in contemporary society;

- curriculum is all planned learnings for which the school is responsible;

- curriculum is the totality of learning experiences provided to students so that they can attain general skills and knowledge at a variety of learning sites;

- curriculum is what the students construct from working with a computer and its various networks, such as the internet;

- curriculum is the questioning of authority and the searching for complex views of human situations.

(Marsh, 2004, pages 4–7)

Examining the body of literature (Kelly, 2009; Schiro, 2008; Ellis, 2004; Kliebard, 2004), it appears that all agree that curriculum is a way of planning and organising the teaching within education.

> *More consistent with such an aim is a curriculum which organises cultural resources in usable forms for the purposes of enabling pupils to deepen and extend their understanding of the problems and dilemmas of everyday life in society, and to make informed and intelligent judgements about how they might be resolved. Such a curriculum will be responsive to a pupil's own thinking and their emerging understandings and insights into human situations. It will therefore be continuously tested, reconstructed and developed by teachers as part of the pedagogical process itself, rather than in advance of it. Hence, the idea of pedagogically driven curriculum change as an innovative experience.*

(Elliott, 1998, page xiii)

Scott addressed the different types of curriculum as they *may refer to a system, as in a national curriculum, an institution, as in the school curriculum, or even to an individual school . . . Its four dimensions are: aims or objectives, content or subject matter and this refers to knowledge, skills or dispositions which are implicit in choice of terms and the way that they are arranged* (Scott, 2008, page 19).

A curriculum includes, as Walker (1990) argues, the fundamental concepts of content, purpose and organisation that are underpinned by pedagogy. Pedagogy is about the values, beliefs, principles and ethics of how knowledge should be constructed and shared among the communities of learners that drive curriculum content, organisation and purpose.

Developing synergy between pedagogy and curriculum

As can be seen from the above discussion, there are clear differences between pedagogy and curriculum. It can be said that pedagogy is the theoretical, conceptual ideas of how to organise teaching and learning, whereas curriculum is the actual organisation of the educational programme. In that sense, pedagogy is the philosophical ideology of the educational setting and this might include teachers, learners and the community, whereas curriculum is the way that the learning is organised in an educational setting.

The examples below try to demonstrate the synergy between pedagogy and curriculum – and highlight the role of observation in the curriculum. They provide an overview of the EYFS and two further well known curricular approaches: Reggio Emilia and Te Whaariki.

Example 1: Early Years Foundation Stage

When we discuss the development of a pedagogy for the early years, the starting point is a search for quality within it. In the EYFS there is an attempt to set the standards for early years practice and the aim is to improve quality. Early years practice is viewed as a partnership between the settings and the parents. The ultimate aim of the EYFS is a standardised practice among early years settings, with parents being assured *that EYFS sets the standards that all early years providers must meet to ensure that children learn and develop well and are kept healthy and safe* (DfE, 2012a, page 2).

The EYFS emphasises four key aspects of early years provision:

- **quality and consistency** *in all early years settings, so that every child makes good progress and no child gets left behind;*

- *a secure foundation through learning and development opportunities which are planned around the needs and interests of each individual child and are assessed and reviewed regularly;*

- **partnership working** *between practitioners and with parents and/or carers;*

- **equality of opportunity** *and anti-discriminatory practice, ensuring that every child is included and supported.*

(DfE, 2012a, page 2)

In order to provide quality in early years education, it is important for professionals and practitioners to understand children's development. To achieve this, four overarching guiding principles are recommended in EYFS:

- *every child is a* **unique child**, *who is constantly learning and can be resilient, capable, confident and self-assured;*

- *children learn to be strong and independent through* **positive relationships**;

- *children learn and develop well in* **enabling environments**, *in which their experiences respond to their individual needs and there is a strong partnership between practitioners and parents and/or carers; and*

- **children develop and learn in different ways and at different rates**. *The framework covers the education and care of all children in early years provision, including children with special educational needs and disabilities.*

(DfE: 2012a, page 3)

The EYFS opened to public debate the issues of what consists effective practice, what exactly should be done in the Early Years sector, and how the optimum programme should be delivered in order to raise the EYFS learning goals. There are two main concerns emerging from examining the standardised principled approach of the EYFS.

Firstly, the standards are linked to the classic developmental approach outcomes in children (the learning and development goals). The priority of the EYFS is to *provide the foundation children need to make the most of their abilities and talents to make the most as they grow up* (DfE, 2012a, page 1). It thus sets a number of early learning and developmental goals that children should have acquired by the end of the academic year in which they reach the age of five (DfE 2012a, DfE 2012b). The developmental approach outcomes in the EYFS leave no space for the child as 'a knower'. Instead, the environment creates the *performer child* where the child needs to perform to outcomes and outputs which are observable and measurable. It follows that practitioners are rated according to these outcomes as criteria for quality.

Secondly, in the EYFS is stated that *it promotes teaching and learning to ensure children's 'school readiness' and gives children the broad range of knowledge and skills that provide the right foundation for good future progress through school and life* (DfE, 2012a, page 2). This approach to the child in the EYFS places value on children in terms of them meeting future goals, standards and learning outcomes. It assumes that children need to progress to the next stage of development, from maybe lesser child to better child. The terms 'development, 'developmental goals' or 'learning goals' invoke a sense that children are not yet developed (whole/holistic) and thus need developing ('improving'), or that there is an existing, pre-determined place at which a child may arrive (presumably school).

Within these views, it is important that the early years workforce is able to implement the EYFS, but also form a voice and a theoretical argument regarding his/her own practice and pedagogical values. The role of the early years workforce should be to:

- lead practice based on a theoretical background;
- stimulate pedagogical discussion among the team, requiring an understanding of current pedagogical practices;
- disseminate and implement current policies within the team.

Reggio Emilia

Reggio Emilia is a community-supported system of early childhood education and care situated in a small town in northern Italy. Loris Malaguzzi introduced an early years system to the Reggio Emilia province, based on his vision of a child as an active, strong and powerful human being. Both Malaguzzi (1995) and his co-worker Rinaldi (1995) based their pedagogy on cognitive ideas of child development. They placed particular emphasis on Vygotsky's ideas – that knowledge is not adopted by the child, but is constructed by the child through interaction with a more mature or experienced peer or adult (Miller *et al.*, 2003).

The originality of Reggio Emilia is that there is no written curriculum. Instead it takes a localised approach to the education of its young children. This approach is free from external and formalised pressures and standards. There are no government objectives or goals to be achieved, and the starting point is the child; consequently the curriculum *emerges* from children's own interests and needs (Rinaldi, 1995). The Reggio Emilia approach to early years pedagogy is developed via a constant dialogue with the early years team, the children and the parents. In this approach, the child is viewed as *rich in potential, strong, powerful, competent and, most of all, connected to adults and other children* (Malaguzzi, 1993, page 10).

The view of the child *rich in potential* underpins the main principles of this pedagogical approach. Learning is viewed as a social activity that involves all participants: parents, children and the local community. Consequently, all of these participants are engaging in constant discussion about the activities in the classes.

Fundamental principles in the Reggio Emilia approach to early years pedagogy are:

- the partnerships with parents and communication with them;

- listening to the *hundred languages* that children use to communicate;

- informal assessment and documentation of children's work as the starting point for discussion among staff, children and parents;

- the physical environment, important in the Reggio Emilia for the emotional stability of the children.

In the Reggio Emilia approach, the early years workforce collects evidence about what the children are involved in. This evidence is documented either in the form of individual portfolios for each child or by photographs, and these become starting points for discussions at weekly team meetings. From these discussions the planning of activities emerges. Ongoing dialogue among the staff, parents, children and the wider community forms the educational programme and its activities, this being a key aspect in the pedagogy.

Fillipini illustrates how Reggio Emilia works: *The 'pedagogista' (early years professional) works with the parents and teachers towards educational aims and goals and has a co-ordinating role with many facets, including administration and training* (Fillipini, 1995, in Miller *et al.*, 2003).

And again, citing Vecchi: *The 'artelier' (or 'artist in residence') is closely involved in project work and in the visual documentation of the children's work* (Vecchi, 1995, in Miller *et al.*, 2003).

Te Whaariki

In the early years settings in New Zealand, there is an attempt to create a multicultural curriculum. This is known as 'Te Whaariki' and is an attempt to describe the nature of the national curriculum. Based on Bronfenbrenner's ideas about the *nested environment* and human development, it contains, as a main principle, the inclusion of beliefs, values and cultural identities of each local community (New Zealand Ministry of Education, 1996).

The Te Whaariki curriculum emphasises children's freedom to choose materials and activities and to take ownership of their own learning. Children are viewed as able *to grow up as competent and confident learners and communicators, healthy in mind, body and spirit, secure in their sense of belonging and in the knowledge that they make a valued contribution to society* (New Zealand Ministry of Education 1996).

The framework of this curriculum is based on children's own interests and aspirations (Tyler, 2002). Similar to the EYFS, there are some principles to guide the early years team.

- Empowerment (*Whakamana*). It is central to the curriculum that the child takes ownership of its own development and learning.

- Holistic development (*Kotahitanga*). The child is viewed as a 'whole'. It is emphasised that the child learns in a holistic way, taking into consideration not only the child's physical, social, emotional and cognitive development, but also the cultural context and the spiritual aspects of the child's environment.

- Family and Community (*Whanau Tangata*). Again, similar to the EYFS partnership, the wider world of family and community is an integral part of the early childhood curriculum.

- Relationships (*Nga Hononga*). Children's interactions with peers, adults and real life objects that enhance their learning.

Teachers using the Te Whaariki framework take into account children's well-being, their sense of belonging, the contributions they make, the importance of communication and opportunities to develop exploration. Furthermore, within this curriculum framework, there is an importance placed on a Maori immersion within the New Zealand curriculum in order to strengthen *Te Reo Maori* – the Maori language. Te Whaariki recognises the distinctive role of an identifiable Maori curriculum that protects Maori culture through the use of Maori language (Carr, 1999).

The five main strands of this pedagogical approach for children and families are to feel that they belong in the community of the early years setting, to ensure that children's and families' well-being is safeguarded, an exploration of the environment, an emphasis on communication and, finally, to ensure that individual (and/or group) contributions are valued. Within this framework Carr (2001) emphasises the importance of assessment as a continuous process based on observations. Carr suggests that through assessing children's experiences early years practitioners can look at whether children are:

- taking an interest;

- coping with change and difference;

- connecting places and experiences;

- finding out new things;

- practising old things;

- tackling difficulty;

- developing relationships with adults;

- developing relationships with peers;

- taking responsibility.   (Carr, 1998, page 15)

Carr (1998) introduces the idea of *learning dispositions*. Learning dispositions are central in the Te Whaariki curriculum and are about encouraging children's positive experiences with knowledge, developing the skills and strategies that children will accumulate and which will help them not only during childhood, but in acquiring skills that will be of benefit throughout the rest of their lives. Thus, assessment is central to this process, in order for early years practitioners to be able to help children to cultivate these dispositions.

It is among the principles of Te Whaariki that children are producing *working theories* about themselves and about the people, places and activities in their lives, and that these working theories *become increasingly useful for making sense of the world, for giving a child control over what happens, for problem solving and for further learning.* (Te Whaariki, 1996, page 44).

What is interesting and important in the Te Whaariki curriculum is the freedom of early years settings to create their own programmes, given a common framework of principles. Each small community has its own culture, traditions and needs, and real world experiences can be transformed within the class. A second important aspect of this curriculum is the emphasis on children's interests and needs. In this way, the metaphorical reference made to weaving by Te Whaariki (woven mat) takes shape. Children's cultural backgrounds, language and interests are an integral part of the early years practice.

Compare these three early years curricula. What similarities and differences can you identify? How can this influence your own practice?

Start this task by identifying how each curriculum views the child, and what philosophical and developmental theories might underpin each of them.

Can you identify the key pedagogical ideas that underpin these curricular approaches?

The curriculum of early years

Since September 2008, the Early Years Foundation Stage (EYFS) became statutory across the early years sector in England. All early years settings hosting children from birth to five years old had to implement the EYFS. In the Ten Years Strategy (DCSF, 2008a) it is stated that the EYFS is not a curriculum; rather, it is a framework to improve early years practice and raise the standards within early years education and care. While the EYFS is a detailed and descriptive practical guidance for the early years sector, the Government stated clearly that it is not to be seen as part of the National Curriculum (DCSF, 2008a). However, issues around the statutory nature of the EYFS (i.e. the assessment profile and the inspection of early years settings across the main principles and outcomes of the EYFS) do not demonstrate a culture of framework and guidance: they are characteristic of a central, pre-described and standardised curriculum. The EYFS nevertheless complies with many definitions of a curriculum in that it has a totality and control of the learning and development assistance provided to children. EYFS is welcomed in the early years sector as mentioned in the introduction of this book, as it is providing a coherent, consistent framework that supports children's learning and development across the early years sector. It focuses on a play-based approach and attempts to embrace children's participation.

I believe that while the current policy context (the EYFS) in which education and care in early childhood are situated is both exciting and challenging, it remains imperative that practitioners rise to the challenge of critically reflecting how they are positioned and how they seek to position themselves and to construct professional identities.

A curriculum in an early years setting should be based around some key principles. To begin with, we are concerned with the experiences of children. These experiences are becoming part of their learning processes and development. Emphasis on the early years curriculum should be based on play. There is a plethora of research emphasising that role play is essential in early years education (Moyles, 1989, 2010; Nutbrown, 2006; Wood and Attfield, 2005; Wood, 2010a, 2010b). They all conclude that children in early years settings need opportunities to initiate their own learning, learn from each other and adults, and pursue their own interests. Play provides children with such an environment and helps them to engage in a number of experiences and materials that advance their development and learning. In early years settings, the curriculum is not a formalised approach to teaching and learning seen in a primary or secondary classroom; through play, children's experiences and interests are exercised and developed.

Secondly, the early years curriculum is concerned with making decisions about the content and the process of children's learning experiences. Based on observations of and reflection on daily activities, the early years workforce is making decisions about a variety of issues and topics that will be explored in the setting and via which children will be able to enjoy a creative and stimulating environment. Any early years setting should therefore have the freedom to plan and provide a broadly-based curriculum which will allow all children to meet their particular developmental and learning needs and develop good attitudes towards their learning.

Finally, another important element of early years curriculum is that it involves many groups. It is important that within EYFS, children's learning and development is viewed as work in partnership. The early years workforce, the children, the parents, the communities and the early years settings should all serve as partners and should all have a voice about how the environment and the activities are organised. Through observation planning of children's development and learning, reflection on the activities and collaboration with parents and other professionals, the curriculum should offer a stimulating environment for children. Thus, what is going on in the classroom is part of a decision-making process from many perspectives.

To conclude, the early years curriculum should be based on a pedagogical ethos where all participants are valued (the professional team, children, parents, communities) and feel equal in the decision-making process. Play should be central as a way for children to interact with the environment and the materials, developing flexibility of thought, trying to solve problems, putting different elements of a situation together in various ways or looking at the world from different viewpoints.

ACTIVITY 2

You have developed an observation plan in order to evaluate the areas in your early years setting. You have used a tracking technique to identify which areas children are using most during the day.

The following figure illustrates the number of children recorded who spent time in different areas of the nursery. Information has been collected over a period of three weeks during play time. Study the figure and think how you can use this to inform your curriculum. Consider:

- *How can this inform future curriculum planning?*

- *Which areas will you enrich?*

- *Which areas might you consider changing?*

- *Which areas might you consider replacing?*

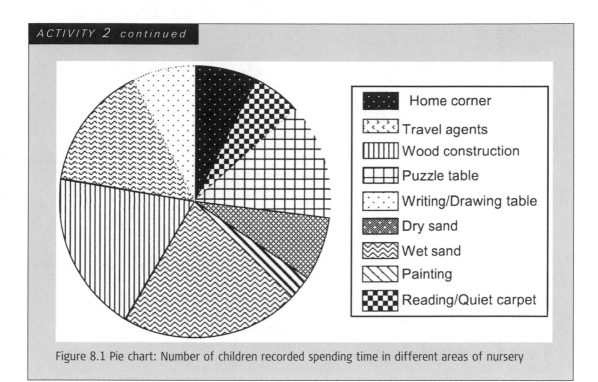

Figure 8.1 Pie chart: Number of children recorded spending time in different areas of nursery

Observing for curriculum

Throughout this book, the importance of observation in early years education has been explored. When observing for curriculum, the early years workforce attempts to inform practice and support children's learning and development. Thus, rigour in observation planning is essential. It should be underpinned by a pedagogical ethos that mirrors the needs of the early years setting, the needs of children, the needs and expectations of parents and those of the community. Observation outcomes have an impact at a number of levels. To begin with, they impact on the content, organisation and purpose of the curriculum. For example, EYFS promotes a positive view of multi-culturalism, reflecting the more diverse needs of our society. The EYFS attempts to create an ethos where all participants (staff, children, parents) are equals and respected for their own identity and to promote anti-discriminatory policies and regulations which aim to respond positively to social and cultural diversity.

Moreover, observation outcomes impact on children's learning and development by informing the development of the curriculum; they impact on parents' expectations and encourage participation. Finally, observation outcomes impact on the community as one of the fundamental aims in education is to develop children who will become active citizens. For example, it was shown that in the Te Whaariki curriculum, observation is a tool for liaising with the community and a way to invite the community into the early years class.

ACTIVITY 3

Examine the curriculum of your early years setting and consider:

- *how you observe and assess children;*
- *how you use observation outcomes to develop your curriculum.*

In this activity, consider how important the following parameters are:

- *your pedagogical ethos;*
- *the needs of your early years setting;*
- *the needs of children;*
- *the needs of parents;*
- *the statutory requirements;*
- *the expertise of your team;*
- *your vision (what you aim to achieve in your setting);*
- *your outcomes in an early years setting.*

Throughout this book it has been suggested that observation is not only an activity that describes what happens between the observer and the observed event/child, but also a process that involves clear aims and objectives, ethical considerations, planning, analysis and documentation. As illustrated in the following figure (Fig. 8.2), linking observation

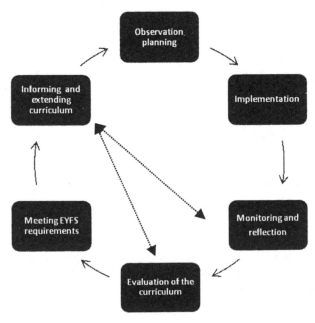

Figure 8.2 Linking observation with the curriculum

planning with the curriculum is about understanding the pedagogical practices that underpin your curriculum and about creating an observation plan where all participants involved understand, share and are able to implement the observation. Analysis of observation helps the monitoring and reflection process in the early years setting as a way of evaluating the curriculum and extending it. When you work in a regulatory framework such as the EYFS, it helps you also to meet the statutory requirements.

Linking observations to the Early Years Foundation Stage

Central to EYFS are the following aims:

- meet the diverse needs of the child;

- promote partnership working;

- provide flexible provision;

- create activities for children through play;

- improve the quality of provision for children.

Among the statutory duties, the Early Years Foundation Stage places emphasis on:

- observation of children, in order to identify their needs, interests and their skills and abilities;

- recording children's responses in different situations;

- an analysis of observation recordings in order to identify children's achievements, or to identify areas where children need further support;

- involving the parents as part of the on-going observation and assessment process (DfE, 2012a , 2012b).

The Early Years Foundation Stage defines assessments of children as being an analysis of what you know about an individual child in terms of that child's development and learning. The purpose of the assessment in the EYFS is to:

- make informed decisions about the child's progress;

- plan your activities to meet the needs of children.

The EYFS suggests two types of assessment:

The first – *Formative Assessments* – are based on observations and use techniques such as photographs, video recordings, children's drawings and information from parents. Observation recordings form a picture of the everyday life of children in the early years setting. They provide rich information for formative evidence on which to base future planning and to extend your knowledge and understanding of how children develop and learn, as well as providing evidence of their developing competencies, persistent interests, dispositions and schemas (Athey, 1990). Therefore it is important for observations to be an integral part of early years practice. Observations are not the final process in a curriculum, but part of the actions of early years professionals and practitioners for constantly improving quality within the setting. Formative assessments based on observation recordings assist the early years practitioner to:

- offer a flexible provision for children, where activities are changed when children lack interest in them and plans are altered to follow children's interests and needs and where new activities take place to rekindle children's interests;

- provide evidence for starting communications with the parents and to encourage parental involvement

- provide evidence for communicating with other services and local authorities.

For effective formative assessment it is important to make observations:

- integral and a regular part of life in the setting;

- incidental, when something is happening outside planned activities;

- during activities with children.

The second type of assessment is *Summative Assessment*. In the EYFS it is a statutory requirement that each child will have a summative assessment at the end of the EYFS. This is a final assessment, which includes a summary of all the formative assessments done over a long period of time, and offers a more holistic picture of a child's development and learning. It is stated in the EYFS (DfE, 2012a) that each profile will include information about the child's progress towards the stated early learning goals.

The summative assessment is as equally important as the formative assessment. It is not only used to communicate with local authorities and for inspection purposes, it is also a very helpful tool as it assists:

- transitions from one early years setting to another and transitions to Key Stage 1;

- professionals and practitioners to evaluate the activities and their implementation;

- approaches to other agencies with informed evidence, if required.

As can be seen in both types of assessment, observations are vital to professionals and practitioners in all areas of early years practice. Observational skills need to be developed from a very early stage in a practitioner's training.

The formative and summative assessments of children are a statutory part of the Assessment and Reporting Arrangements within the EYFS.

CASE STUDY

Alice is three years and 11 months. One emphasis in the EYFS is the effective transition in and out of it. Her records show that there are some concerns with her transition from playgroup to nursery at a social development level. After implementing an observation plan, you have discovered that she has found the change quite difficult to manage. Alice is not integrating with the other children. She shows anxiety when her mother brings her into the nursery. She displays some introvert behaviour and, although she engages with adults, she does not like to make contact or conversations with the other children, nor does she play with them.

- How can you plan your curriculum in helping Alice to interact with the other children?

- What observation techniques will you use?

- How are you going to analyse your findings? How are you going to document them?

- How are you going to share your findings with her parents?

- How is what you have learnt going to influence your curriculum practice?

In your planning, consider which behaviours you will observe and what your aims and objectives will be. In the light of your findings, consider how the team meeting will proceed and how you are going to investigate whether Alice has any other additional needs.

Think about how the observation process you have designed will assist you to:

- assess the educational programme, in terms of how it will help Alice to interact with other children;

- share information with her parents;

- share information with Alice in an appropriate manner.

SUMMARY

This chapter aimed to revisit the discussion of pedagogy and identify the differences between pedagogy and curriculum. In an early years setting, we do need clear pedagogical approaches in order to design and implement an effective curriculum for children's learning and development. A curriculum for early childhood education should be driven by play and be appropriate to children's stages of learning and development but at the same time provide an environment where it enriches their learning and stimulates them for further development.

There followed an attempt to reflect on the EYFS by drawing examples from international curriculum practices, such as Reggio Emilia and Te Whaariki.

From the EYFS, the Reggio Emilia and Te Whaariki approaches, we can see that wherever there is formally written or unwritten, informal curricula, observation appears to be the

SUMMARY *continued*

main tool for early years practitioners. In some curricula, like EYFS, the monitoring process of children is more formalised in terms of assessment, whilst in others (such as Reggio Emilia or Te Whaariki) it is less formal and less standardised. However, within each curriculum approach, in order to monitor/assess children's progress, as well as to evaluate the educational programme itself, there is a need for rigour and systematic observation planning.

*FURTHER
READING*

For more on the early years curriculum:

Kelly, AV (2009) *The Curriculum: Theory and Practice* (6th ed.). London: SAGE.

Palaiologou, I (ed.) (2012) *Early Years Foundation Stage: Theory and Practice.* London: SAGE.

Rodger, R (2012) *Planning an Appropriate Curriculum in the Early Years: A guide for early years practitioners and leaders, students and parents.* London: Routledge.

For more on the importance of play:

Edmiston, B (2008) *Forming Ethical Identities in Early Childhood Play.* London: Routledge.

Moyles, J (ed.) (2010) *Thinking about Play; Developing a Reflective Approach.* Maidenhead: Open University Press.

Summary: Early years workforce and observation

Through reading this chapter, you should be able to reflect on:

- your role within the early years learning environment;

- your role with regard to current policy and legislation;

- your role within the early years workforce and the implementation of the Early Years Foundation Stage.

This chapter summarises the main role of observation for the early years workforce. It looks at the role of the early years workforce in the context of policy, and of their role as educators for young children. It highlights the importance of observations as a means of implementing policies, as well as of understanding children, and in creating appropriate learning environments for them. Although observation is a valid tool, there are nevertheless some limitations.

The policy context of the early years workforce

In the introductory chapter, it became clear that services for children and families have been changing, as have quality standards for the early years sector. Even as this book goes to print, a number of changes are taking place. The EYFS has now been revised and the qualifications framework for the early years workforce is under review. As mentioned in the Introduction, Cathy Nutbrown's interim report published in March 2012 has stressed that there is a need to improve qualifications in the early years sector. The Early Years Professional Status, which was part of a wider Labour Government plan for children's services, is also under re-consultation. In 2006, the Common Core of Skills and Knowledge set out basic standards that practitioners in the children's workforce needed in order to work effectively with children and families (HM Government, 2006a). It aimed at developing a framework of skills that would help all practitioners to meet the *working together* philosophy. The skills and knowledge required can be described under six headings:

- effective communication and engagement with children, young people and families;

- children's and young people's development;

- safeguarding and promoting the welfare of the child;

- supporting transitions;

- multi-agency working;

- sharing information.

The Government has announced that they expect all people working in the field of children's services and supporting families to have a basic level of competence in these six areas of the Common Core (HM Government, 2006a). Under the 'Child and Young People's Development' section, two of the main skills which should be demonstrated are good observation and good judgement. The development of the postgraduate (Level 7) qualification – the National Professional Qualification for Integrated Children's Centre Leadership (NPQICL) – for practitioners who lead the multi-professional Children's Centres and the National Standards for Children's Centre Leaders *are distinct from but complementary to those . . . for Early Years Professionals* (DfES, 2007), but share the requirement to demonstrate skills in observation and judgement.

In an era of change, the early years workforce is undergoing yet more development. The role of the early years workforce in the context of policy development is both challenging and multi-dimensional. The creation and implementation of the Early Years Professional Status had become central to defining a clear career structure for people entering the sector. It was intended that the Early Years Professional Status would provide sufficient staff with appropriate skills to deliver the Early Years Foundation Stage, in order to raise and ensure the quality of provision. The role of the professional has a dual purpose. On the one hand, to ensure that policies, legislation, regulatory standards and ethical concerns are met, as well as to ensure that they promote partnership working. Additionally, the professional has an accountability to deliver the outcomes of the EYFS and the ECM.

Although the EYPS and the EYFS are positive developments in raising quality in the early years, there is some confusion and uncertainty among professionals. Firstly, it has been suggested that the EYPS will have equivalency with qualified teachers and confer a recognised status, yet it is not a formal qualification. This might lead to a lowering of aspirations among people who are keen to work in the sector, but who feel uncertain about training to acquire a 'status' but not a 'qualification'.

Evidence from research which focused on early years practice and pedagogy (Moyles *et al.*, 2001; Sylva *et al.*, 2001; Siraj-Blatchford and Sylva, 2002; Taylor Nelson Sofres with Aubrey, 2002; Sylva *et al.*, 2004; OECD, 2011; Owen and Haynes, 2010; Allen, 2011) emphasised that children's cognitive outcomes and learning achievements related positively to adult planned and initiated activities, to shared thinking between adults, children and parents and to the level of qualifications of the early years workforce. It is now recognised that there is a necessity for well-qualified early years practitioners and professionals to have a sound theoretical background following the suggested principles of the EYFS, have a deep understanding of children's development and needs and to be recognised as professional practitioners within the early years. Children's development and learning is enhanced in an environment where professionals are able to observe children's development and to analyse these recordings as means of evaluating their activities, and therefore subsequently creating opportunities for furthering children's learning experiences.

The aims of the EYFS are to raise quality, to promote equality of opportunity, to encourage partnership work, to improve safety and security and to consider the child and his or her environment (such as in the family setting), and these aims are central. The EYP is asked to deliver all of these aims in a successful way.

There arise two potential problems, the first of which is the inevitably increased workload of the workforce. Secondly, the implementation of a formalised structured curriculum may become a trap for the early years workforce as, in an attempt to meet requirements, the developmental and learning needs of children may be ignored; implementation of the EYFS in the light of formalised inspection might become a priority, and not the children themselves.

Finally, a wealth of research in the field of the multi-agency and inter-agency work (Roaf and Lloyd, 1995; Watson, Townsley and Abbott, 2002; Puonti, 2004; Warmington *et al.*, 2004) indicates that crossing professional boundaries in order to work together for effective children's practice is a complex issue. It requires a learning process that takes place within the settings and requires the development of a common work culture and an acknowledgment of tension and contradictions. The development of a Common Core Skills and Knowledge aims to ease these tensions. However, Brown and White (2006) found that in the *joining up* philosophy of the children's services there are certain limitations for successful integration, such as financial boundaries, cultural differences among profes-sionals, a lack of clarity for roles and responsibilities and a lack of clarity around issues of leadership. They conclude their study by questioning the *joining up* work ethos with children and emphasise *the complexities of integrated working are unlikely to be overcome to produce its indented benefits unless a clear and sustained focus on the long-term outcomes for clients is maintained* (Brown and White, 2006).

Although there are positive changes and encouraging moves towards raising quality in the early years, there is a doubtful and uncertain (as well as confusing) context. The early years workforce is asked to become both *expert* in implementing legislation and a *specialised* educator in order to deliver the outcomes of the EYFS. It is also asked to become an *agent of change* in the integrated services and to communicate with other children's workforce staff on an on-going basis.

The following sections discuss the role of the early years workforce in terms of policy context and in terms of their role as educators, to highlight how observation can become a tool towards effective practice and partnerships.

The role of the early years workforce in the policy context

As mentioned above, an important aspect of the early years workforce role is to have a good knowledge and understanding of the policy context and to be able to understand how this influences practice. Currently, the outcomes of the Every Child Matters agenda are the main aims that will dominate your work. However, as changes in the policy occur, the early years professional should be able to search for these changes and keep up to date with all the relevant information. Accessing government websites regularly is important. The early years workforce is not only responsible for keeping up to date with current legislations and policies, but also to inform the team that he or she works in line with them.

The early years workforce is responsible for:

- implementing the Early Years Foundation Stage (the statutory duties and the pedagogical aspects of the EYFS);
- developing play-based learning;
- promoting the holistic development of children;
- ensuring that all children and their families are treated equally and that diversity is promoted;
- preparing all the documentation for inspections;
- the safety of children;
- promoting the well-being and health of children;
- promoting effective staff interactions;
- being able to achieve inter-agency work;
- establishing partnerships with families and other services;
- meeting quality standards.

ACTIVITY 1

Looking at the above list, can you add any other responsibilities?

In meeting the Every Child Matters' five outcomes, as mentioned in Chapter 2, the Common Assessment Framework is central to identifying any additional needs of children. There is an emphasis on a common process that enables practitioners to undertake an assessment, to which different services and sectors will contribute. For this purpose, there is a common form and a common pre-assessment checklist, to help practitioners and professionals record all the relevant information. The areas covered are:

- development;
- health;
- family and social relationships;
- self-care skills, independence and learning;
- safety and protection;
- emotional warmth and stability.

All these areas are regarded as equally important for a child's well-being. Within this framework, the early years workforce has a key role. In everyday practice the early years workforce needs to make sure that all children under his or her supervision are meeting the above areas and to decide whether or not any additional needs have arisen that need to be addressed. As pointed out in Chapter 2, observations are a useful tool in identifying any needs by collecting pertinent evidence on children's progress. For the effective implementation of the e-CAF, observations are central. Although there are pre-assessment checklists, as well as standardised forms, these alone cannot become independent tools for collecting evidence. As discussed in Chapter 3, when we observe children we try to collect accurate information and specific evidence of what has been seen happening. Consequently, identifying additional needs for the effective implementation of the e-CAF requires the use of a variety of observation techniques, in order to collect information which, after analysis, will lead us to conclude whether the e-CAF is required or not.

As can be seen in the context of policy, observations are a key function for effective implementation. Systematic observation can provide the early years professional with valid information in order to put the CAF to effective use.

Moreover, observations can function as a useful communication tool with other professionals. Having collected a wealth of evidence, the required forms can be completed and additional information can also be provided if it is required.

The early years workforce will master certain observation skills that can be used in other contexts. Observation skills that will develop, originally to observe children and the educational programme and its activities, can be transferred to situations where the early years workforce will be asked to work either in an inter-agency or a multi-agency environment. Observing the way other professionals work and listening to the language they use, may benefit your own work in terms of reflecting on your own practice. Being able to wait and collect evidence will help you to communicate better, and observing and analysing how other professionals work might become a helpful tool to furthering your understanding when you have to work with others. A difference of opinion within multi-agency and inter-agency work is one of the main problems you might have to face within the 'joined up' policy context and when the e-CAF is implemented. Your observation skills can become your tool, as you will use them to gain an insight into how other sectors operate.

The role of observation in the context of policy is dualistic. On the one hand, as previously stated, it can facilitate the early years workforce to implement policies. On the other hand, systematic observation (which includes the analysis of findings, to inform the EYP's own practice) can help to develop a critical approach to policies and can influence practice, policy and legislation.

One of the main responsibilities of the early years workforce is the delivery of the Early Years Foundation Stage. It is a statutory duty for the early years workforce to collect evidence, in order to complete the Assessment Scales and the eProfile. These assessments will be used for assessing children's progress, to share information, to promote partnership and for inspection purposes. Central to this statutory process is observation as a valid tool, in order to collect all the evidence that you need for the effective completion of these assessment scales. Through observations you can develop a critical approach to them and can voice your opinion to communicate with either other early years professionals or other services:

> Clear, positive communication to staff is particularly essential when they are busy with the 'day job' and when change has not impacted on them yet. The two-way communication, through for instance regular learning labs, is crucial to gain staff trust and create and maintain motivation.

(Bachmann et al. 2006, page 9)

Observation findings can also be used in your own setting for informal training and staff development purposes. They can enhance and strengthen the links within the team (team building) and they can become the starting point to discuss critically and reflect on your activities and practice. Team meetings can become more effective with observation findings, as you build the discussion upon evidence gathered.

The role of the early years workforce as educators and observers

The early years setting is a context which children can enjoy, being occupied in activities which stimulate them and which help them to develop skills. In such environments, the practitioners and professionals perform the role of facilitators of children's learning and development. The practitioners and the early years professional should provide an environment where children make progress, taking into consideration children's equality, diversity and inclusion, so enabling children from different cultural backgrounds to interact with one another and share different experiences.

In such an environment, the early years workforce should demonstrate the different facets of the role of educator, use appropriate language, respect values and practices and praise and encourage all children. As the facilitator, the early years workforce has a good understanding of children's development and pedagogy, and of how these are both linked to their everyday practice with children. As mentioned in Chapter 1, working in early years requires an understanding of the different views of children that form and underpin practice, a good understanding of how children develop, and the different theoretical approaches to this development. This specialised knowledge is not isolated from the development of pedagogy through reflection and evaluation of current theories alone.

One of the common findings of different research projects on pedagogy in the early years (Moyles et al., 2001; Sylva et al., 2001; Siraj-Blatchford and Sylva, 2002; Taylor Nelson Sofres with Aubrey, 2002; Miller et al., 2010; Pugh, 2010; Brooker et al., 2010) stresses the fact that in settings where children's learning is most enhanced, the practitioners focus on child-initiated activities and planning and where resourcing and assessment are integrated into daily practice. The important tool for planning and assessment is observation. As mentioned in Chapter 2, observations should be part of the daily routine of the early years setting. Everyday observations of children's interactions, their progress within the activities and the analysis of the observation recordings, all help the Early Years Workforce to make links between theory and practice, and inevitably to modify their pedagogical principles. For example, in Chapter 1, where Piagetian and Vygotskian ideas were discussed, observations of children's activities were presented to demonstrate how theory is applied in practice.

Moreover, the EYFS is stressing the holistic approach to children's development. In Chapter 6, this view was extended to observations and to children's assessment. To develop a pedagogy that meets the requirements of a holistic approach to children, observations become the means to understand children and parents' diversity, values and beliefs, and the wider cultural context that children and parents live in and are influenced by. This wider context is not isolated from life in an early years setting. Children's experiences in the family context are inter-linked with children's experiences in the early years setting. In this respect, the role of early years workforce as educators and now as an educator has great value. The early years workforce needs to develop a portfolio of skills and attitudes and to be able to use these skills to develop practice and to be able to understand the wider context in which children are raised. The early years workforce needs to listen to children attentively. Powerful tools for this are observations, as they further our understanding and deepen our knowledge of children.

In Chapter 1, conditions for learning were discussed, emphasising children's development, play, children's needs, their freedom to choose materials and activities and their ownership of learning. As explained in Chapter 2, observations offer rich information about children's learning, which enable the early years workforce to inform future planning and pedagogy. Observations are starting points for sharing information among the team, but in the role of early years workforce as educators these can become evidence for, and inform, pedagogy and the educational programme and its activities.

In Chapter 2, it was demonstrated that observations can be used to:

- find out about children as individuals;

- monitor their progress;

- inform curriculum planning;

- enable staff to evaluate the provisions they make;

- provide a focus for discussion and improvement;

- understand early years practice better;

- ensure their conclusions are 'woven' into early years daily practice.

All these are important aspects for the everyday practice of the early years workforce, as it helps to:

- assess children's development and learning (which is statutory in the EYFS);

- assess and evaluate the early years programme and activities in order to inform practice;

- share this information with children in an appropriate manner for their age;

- share this information with parents;

- share this information with local authorities;

- retain this information for the purposes of inspection;

- share this information with other practitioners, to exchange ideas and to learn from each other.

The observation process as a tool in early years practice assists professionals in developing their specialised knowledge, to gain a deeper understanding of pedagogy and to expand upon pedagogical practices.

The role of early years workforce as educators and not educator is not isolated or distinct from the role of the early years workforce in the context of policy. These are inter-linked roles, and observation skills can become a method for embracing the policy of the educational programme, in order to effectively provide for children.

Closing note

This chapter discussed the role of the early years workforce in the two main contexts in which it works, in relation to observations: the policy context and the educational context. It attempted to summarise key themes that were addressed throughout this book in relation to the role of the early years workforce.

As it undergoes consultation towards a framework which aims to have common standards among all those working in the field, there is a need to establish a professional identity with clear roles and responsibilities. The existing policy documentation helps the early years professional to understand the legal context of this. The Early Years Foundation Stage offers a framework for staff to deliver the educational programme in relation to developmental learning goals.

Although there is confusion, anxiety and uncertainty, observation skills will be needed for the early years professional, irrespective of whether or not training will change in the future.

In the positive development of creating a workforce for children, this is equally important and challenging. The training of the early years workforce is about offering positive attitudes and skills for working with young children. The standards proposed by governments define national expectations.

Observations have two main roles – firstly to help you to develop your practice in the educational context and, secondly, to offer skills to overcome the barriers and the problems of multi-agency work. Observations are a way of developing tools for thinking, whereby systematically collecting evidence and analysing this helps you to communicate ideas at a pedagogical level with the other team members. This is necessary in order to meet the goals of the Early Years Foundation Stage, as well as, at a policy level, to communicate ideas with other professionals with whom you will need to collaborate to meet policy outcomes.

FURTHER READING

For more on developing an understanding of policy and practice:

Billington, T (2006) *Working with Children.* London: SAGE.

Miller, L and Cable, C (2010) *Professionalisation, Leadership and Management in the Early Years.* London: SAGE.

Nutbrown, C (2006) *Key Concepts in Early Childhood Education and Care.* London: SAGE.

WEBSITES

To keep up to date with developments in government policy, workforce qualifications and any changes in the Early Years Foundation Stage visit:

WDC website: **www.cwdcouncil.org.uk/**

UK Department for Education: **www.education.gov.uk**

For information on development and support on issues around curriculum working in partnership with parents:

www.foundationyears.org.uk

References

Abbot, L and Nutbrown, C (2001) *Experiencing Reggio Emilia: implications for pre-school provision.* Maidenhead: Open University Press.

Ainsworth, MDS (1969) Object Relations, Dependency, and Attachment: A Theoretical Review of the Infant-Mother Relationship, in *Child Development*, 40: 969–1025.

Ainsworth, MDS (1973) The development of infant-mother attachment, in Cardwell, B and Ricciuti, H (eds.) *Review of child development research* (Vol. 3, 1–94). Chicago: University of Chicago Press.

Ainsworth, MDS (1979) Attachment as related to mother-infant interaction, in *Advances in the Study of Behaviour*, 9: 2–52.

Ainsworth, MDS (1985) Attachments across the life span, in *Bulletin of the New York Academy of Medicine*, 61: 792–812.

Ainsworth, MDS (1989) Attachment beyond infancy, in *American Psychologist*, 44: 709–716.

Ainsworth, MDS and Bell, SM (1970) Attachment, Exploration and Separation: Illustrated by the Behaviour of One-Year-Olds in a Strange Situation, in *Child Development*, 41: 49–67.

Ainsworth, MDS, Blehar, MC, Wates, E and Wall, S (1978) *Patterns of attachment: A psychological study of the strange situation.* Hillsdale, NJ: Erlbaum.

Ainsworth, MDS and Bowlby, J (1991) An Ethological Approach to Personality Development, in *American Psychologist*, 46: 333–341.

Ainsworth, MDS, Bell, SM and Stayton, DJ (1971) Individual differences in the strange situation behaviour of one-year-olds, in Schaffer, HR (ed.) *The origins of human social relations*, 15–71. New York: Academic Press.

Ainsworth, MDS, Bell, SM, Blehar, MC and Main, M (1971) *Physical contact: A study of infant responsiveness and its relation to maternal handling.* Paper presented at the biennial meeting of the Society for Research in Child Development, Minneapolis, MN.

Ainsworth, MDS, Blehar, MC, Waters, E and Wall, S (1978) *Patterns of attachment: A study of the strange situation.* Hillsdale, NJ: Erlbaum.

Alderson, P (2000) Children as researchers. The effect on participation rights on research methodology, in Christensen, P and James, A (eds.) (2000) *Research with children.* New York: Falmer Press.

Alderson, P (2004) Ethics, in Fraser, S, Lewis, V, Ding, S, Kellet, M and Robinson, C (eds.) (2004) *Doing research with children and young people.* London: SAGE.

Allen, G (2011) *Early Intervention: The Next Steps*, available at **www.dwp.gov.uk/docs/early-intervention-next-steps.pdf** (accessed 18 January 2012).

Amstrong, D, Gosling, JW and Marteau, T (1997) The place of inter-rater reliability in qualitative research: an empirical study, in *Sociology*, vol. 31, (3): 597–606.

Anderson, J (1983) *The Architecture of Cognition.* Cambridge, MA: Harvard University.

Aries, P (1962) *Centuries of Childhood. A Social History of Family Life.* Random House.

Athey, C (1990) *Extending Thought in Young Children.* London: Paul Chapman.

Bachmann, M, Husbands, C and O'Brian, M (2006) *National Evaluation of Children's Trust: Managing Change for Children through Children's Trust.* Norwich: University of East Anglia/National Children's Bureau.

Bandura, A (1971) *Psychological modelling.* New York: Lieber-Atherton.

Bandura, A (1977) *Social learning theory.* Englewood Cliffs, NJ: Prentice Hill.

Bandura, A (1986) *Social Foundations of thought and action: A social cognitive theory.* Englewood Cliffs, NJ: Prentice Hall.

Bandura, A (1989) Social cognitive theory, in Vasta, R (ed.) (1989) *Annals of child development: Theories of child development: Revised Foundations and current issues* (vol 6: 1-60). Greenwich, CT: JAI Press.

Bandura, A (2001) Social cognitive theory: An agentic perspective, in *Annual Review of Psychology*, 52: 1-26.

Barad, KK (2007) *Meeting the Universe Halfway: Quantum Physics and the Entanglement of Matter and Meaning.* Durham, NG: Duke University Press.

Bassey, A (1990) On the nature of research in education (part 1), in *Research Intelligence*, BERA newsletter no. 36, pp 35-8.

Bassey, M (1999) *Case Study Research in Educational Settings.* Buckingham: Open University.

Beardsworth, A (1980) Analysing Press Content: Some Technical and Methodological Issues, in sociology review monograph, 29 pp 371-95.

Beaty, J (2006) *Observing for Development in Young Children* (6th ed.). New Jersey: Pearson Merrill Prentice Hall.

Benjamin, AC (1994) Observations in Early Childhood Classrooms: Advice from the field, in *Young Children*. 49 (6): 14-20.

Benton, M (1996) The image of childhood: Representations of the Child in Painting and Literature, 1700-1900, in *Children's Literature in Education*, vol 27, 1: 35-61.

Berk, LE (1997) *Child Development* (4th ed.). London: Allyn and Bacon.

Bernstein, B (1975) *Class, Codes and Control. Volume 3: Towards a Theory of Class, Codes and Control.* London: Routledge.

Bernstein, B (1990) *The Structuring of Pedagogic Discourse. Volume IV.*

Bernstein, B (1996) *Pedagogy, Symbolic Control and Identity. Theory, Research, Critique.* London: Taylor & Francis.

Bernstein, B (2003) Towards a Theory of Class, Codes and Control. *Educational Transmission.* London: Routledge and Kegan Paul.

Bernstein NB (1971) *Class, Codes and Control: Volume 1. Theoretical Studies.*

Bernstein, R (1985) *Habermas and Modernity.* Oxford: Policy Press.

Bick, E (1964) Notes on Infant observation in psychoanalytical training, in *Psychoanalytical Study of Child*, vol. 45: 558-566.

Billington, T (2006) *Working with Children.* London: SAGE.

Bloch, M (1992) Critical perspectives on the historical relationship between child development and early childhood research, in S. Kessler and B. Swadener (1992) (eds.) *Reconceptualising the early childhood curriculum.* New York: NY teachers College Press.

Bourdieu, P (1977) *Outline of a Theory of Practice.* Cambridge: Cambridge University Press.

Bowlby, J (1958). The Nature of the Child's Tie to His Mother. *International Journal of Psychoanalysis*, 39: 350-371.

Bowlby, J (1969) *Attachment.* Attachment and loss. Vol. I. London: Hogarth.

Bowlby, J (1969) *Attachment and Loss: Vol II. Separation, anxiety, anger.* New York: Basic Books.

Bowlby, J (1973) *Separation: Anxiety & Anger.* Attachment and Loss (Vol. 2); (International psycho-analytical library no.95). London: Hogarth Press.

Bowlby, J (1980). *Loss: Sadness & Depression.* Attachment and Loss (Vol. 3); (International psycho-analytical library no.109). London: Hogarth Press.

Bowlby, J (1980) *Attachment and Loss: Vol III, Loss, sadness, and depression.* New York: John Wiley.

Bowlby, J (1986) (December 1986). 'Citation Classic, *Maternal Care and Mental Health*' (**www.garfield.library.upenn.edu/classics1986/A1986F063100001.pdf**) (accessed November 2008).

Bowlby, J (1999) *Attachment.* Attachment and Loss Vol. I (2nd ed.). New York: Basic Books, LCCN 00266879; NLM 8412414.

Bowlby, J (2005) *The Making and Breaking of Affectional Bonds.* Routledge Classics.

Bradford, M (2012) *Planning and Observation of Children Under Three.* London: David Futon Book.

Brandon, M, Salter, C, Warren, C, Dagely, V, Howe, A, and Black, J (2006) *Evaluating the Common Assessment Framework and the Lead Professional Guidance and Implementation in 2005–6* Research Brief RB740 April 2006, Annesley, Notts: DfES Publications.

Brewer, J and Hunter, A (1989) *Multimethod Research: A Synthesis of Styles.* Newbury Park, CA: Sage.

Brewer, J and Hunter, A (2006) *Foundations of Multimethod Research: Synthesizing Styles.* (2nd ed.). London: Sage.

Bronfenbrenner, U (1977) Towards experimental ecology of human development, in *American Psychologist,* 32: 513–531.

Bronfenbrenner, U (1979) *The ecology of human development.* Cambridge, MA: Harvard University Press.

Bronfenbrenner, U (1989) Ecological systems theory, in Vasta, R (ed.) (1989) *Annals of child development: Theories of child development: Revised Foundations and current issues,* vol 6: 187–251, Greenwich, CT: JAI Press.

Bronfenbrenner, U (1995) The bioecological model from life course perspective: Reflections of a participant observer, in Moen, P, Elder, GH and Jr. and Luscher, K (eds.) *Examining lives in context* (599–618). Washington DC: American Psychological Association.

Bronfenbrenner, U (2005) *Making human beings human.* Thousand Oaks, CA: SAGE.

Brooker, L, Rogers, S, Ellis, D, Hallett, E and Roberts-Holmes, G (2010) *Practitioner's Experiences of the Early Years Foundation Stage.* DFE-RB029.

Brown, K and White, K (2006) Exploring *the Evidence Base for Integrated Children's Services,* **www.scotland.gov.uk/Publications/2006/01/24120649/1** (accessed 25 November 2007).

Brownlee, J (2004) Teacher's education students' epistemological beliefs: Developing a relational model of teaching, in *Research in Education,* vol. 72 (1): 1–17.

Bruce, T (1997) *Early childhood education* (2nd ed.) London: Hodder and Stoughton.

Bruce, T (2006) *Early childhood: A guide for students.* London: SAGE.

Bruner, JS (1972) *Early Childhood Education.* London: Hodder and Stoughton.

Bruner, JS (1977) Introduction, in Tizard, B and Harvey, D (eds.) *The biology of play.* London: Spastics International Medical Publications.

Bruner, JS (1996) *The Culture of Education,* Cambridge, MA: Harvard University Press.

Bryman, A (1992) *Quantity and quality in social research.* London: Routledge.

Bryman, A (2001) *Social Research Methods.* Oxford: Oxford University Press.

Bryman, A (2004) *Social Research Methods* (2nd edition). Oxford: Oxford University Press.

Bryman, A and Burgess, RG (1999) Introduction: Qualitative Research Methodology: A review, in Bryman, A and Burgess, RG (eds.) *Qualitative Research.* London: SAGE.

Carr, M (1998) *Assessing Children's Learning in Early Childhood Settings: A development programme for discussion and reflection.* Wellington: New Zealand Council for Educational Research.

Carr, M (1999) *Learning and Teaching Stories: New Approaches to Assessment and Evaluation,* **www.aare.edu.au/99pap/pod99298.htm** (accessed December 07)

Carr, M (2001) *Assessment in Early Childhood Settings.* London: Paul Chapman Publishing.

Charmaz, K (2000) Grounded theory: Objectivist and Constructivist Methods, in Denzin, NK and Lincoln, YS (eds.) *Handbook of Qualitative Research* (2nd ed.) (535–597), Thousand Oaks, CA: SAGE.

Christensen, P and James, A (2008) *Research with Children: Perspectives and Practices* (2nd ed.). London: Routledge.

Clark, A (2004) *Listening as a Way of Life.* London: National Children's Bureau.

Clark, A (2005a) Listening to and involving young children: a review of research in practice, in Clark, A, Kjorholt, AT and Moss P (eds.) (2005) *Beyond listening to children on early childhood services.* Bristol: Policy Press.

Clark, A (2005b) Listening to and involving young children: a review of research and practice, in *Early Child Development and Care,* vol 175 (6): 489–505.

Clark, A and Moss, P (2001) *Listening to young children: The Mosaic approach.* London: National Children's Bureau.

Clark, A and Moss, P (2005) *Spaces to Play: More listening to young children using the Mosaic approach.* London: National Children's Bureau.

Clark, A and Moss, P (2006) *Listening to Children: The Mosaic Approach.* London: National Children's Bureau and Joseph Rountree Foundation.

Clark, A, Kjorholt, AT and Moss, P (2005) *Beyond Listening: children's perspectives on early childhood services.* Bristol: The Policy Press.

Cole, DR (2011) *Educational life-forms: Deleuzian Teaching and Practice.* The Netherlands: Sense Publishers.

CWDC (Children's Workforce Development Council) (2006) Early Years Professional National Standards. Leeds: CWDC.

CWDC (2007) *Guidance to the standards for the award of Early Professional Status.* Leeds: CWDC.

CWDC (Children's Workforce Development Council) (2011) Early Years Workforce – the way forward. http://dera.ioe.ac.uk/14028/1/Early_Years_Workforce_-_A_Way_Forward_-_CWDC.pdf (Accessed April 17 2012).

Dahlberg, G (1991) Empathy and social control. On parent-child relations in context of modern childhood, paper presented at the ISSBD Conference.

Dahlberg, G and Moss, P (2010) Introduction by series editors, in Taguchi, HL *Going beyond the theory/practice divide in early childlhood education: Introducing intra-active pedagogy.* London: Routledge.

Dahlberg, G, Moss, P and Pence, A (1999) *Beyond quality in early childhood education and care: Postmodern perspectives.* London: Falmer Press.

Datta, L (1994) Paradigm wars: A basis for peaceful coexistence and beyond, in Reichart CS and Rallis, SF (eds.) *The qualitative-quantitative debate: New perspectives.* San Francisco: Jossey-Bass.

David, T (1993) Educating Children under 5 in the UK, in David, T (ed.), *Educational Provision for our Youngest Children, European Perspectives.* London: Paul Chapman.

Davies, B (1994) On the neglect of pedagogy in education studies and its consequences, in *British Journal of In-Service,* vol 20 (1): 17–34.

DCSF (2008a) *Statutory Framework for the Early Years Foundation Stage.* Nottingham: DCSF.

DCSF (2008b) *Practice Guidance for the Early Years Foundation Stage: Setting the Standards for Learning, Development and Care for Children from Birth to Five.* Nottingham: DCSF.

Deacon, D, Bryman, A and Fenton, N (1998) Collision or Collusion? A discussion of the unplanned triangulation of qualitative and quantitative research methods, in *International Journal of Social Research Methodology*, vol. 21: 5–31.

Dedicott, W (1988). *The Educational Value of Written and Oral Storying.* in Reading, 22 (2): 89–95.

Delouze, G (1990) *The Logic of Sense.* New York: Columbia University Press.

Delouze, G (1994) *Difference and Repetition*, New York: Columbia University Press.

Delouze, G (2001) *Pure Immanence: Essays on a Life* (trans. Anne Boyman). New York: Zone Books.

Denzin, NK (1970) *The research act in sociology: A theoretical introduction to sociological methods.* London: The Butterworth Group.

Department for Education (DfE) (2012a) *Statutory Framework of the Early Years Foundation Stage: Setting the standards for learning, development and care for children from birth to five.* London: DfE.

Department for Education (DfE) (2012b) *Development Matters in the Early Years Foundation Stage* (EYFS). London: DfE.

Derrida, J (1992) *The Other Heading: Reflections on Today's Europe.* Bloomington: Indiana University Press.

Devereux, J (2003) Observing Children, in Devereux, J and Miller, L (eds.) *Working with children in the early years* (2003) (181–202). London: David Fulton Publishers Ltd.

Dewey, J (1995) *Experience and Nature.* Dover Publications.

Dewey, J (1997a) *Democracy and Education: An Introduction to the Philosophy of Education.* Free Press.

Dewey, J (1997b) *Experience and Education.* New York: Touchstone.

Dewsberry, DA (1992). Comparative psychology and ethology: A reassessment. *in American Psychologist*, 47: 208–215.

DfES (1990) *The Rumbold Report*, DfES Publications.

DfES (2003) *Every Child Matters.* London: HMSO.

DfES (2004) *Every Child Matters: Change for Children*, Nottingham: DfES Publications.

DfES (2006) *Common Assessment Framework*, Available at: **www.everychildmatters.gov.uk/deliveringservices/caf/** (accessed 28 September 2007).

Dixon, RA and Learner, RM (1992) A history of systems in developmental psychology, in Bronstein, MH and Lamb, ME (eds.) *Developmental psychology: An advanced textbook* (3rd ed., 3–58).

Dockett, S and Perry, B (2003) Children's voices in research on starting school, paper presented at the Annual Conference of the *European Early Childhood Education Research Association*, Glasgow, September 2003.

Dockett, S and Perry, B (2005) Researching with children: insight from the starting school research project, in *Early Child Development and Care*, vol 175, (6): 507–522.

Dockett, S, Einarsdottir, J and Perry, B (2011) Balancing methodologies and methods in researching with young children, in Harcourt, D, Perry, B and Waller, T (2011) *Researching Young Children's Perspectives: Debating the ethics and dilemmas of education research with children.* London: Routledge.

Dollard, J and Miller, NE (1950). *Personality and psychotherapy.* New York: McGraw-Hill.

Dowling, M (2005) *Young Children's Personal, Social and Emotional Development* (2nd ed.). London: Paul Chapman.

Driscoll, V and Rudge, C (2005) Channels for listening to young children in A Clark, AT Kjorhourt and P Moss (eds.) *Beyond Listening.* Bristol: The Policy Press.

Drummond, MJ (1993) *Assessing Children's Learning* (1st ed.). London: David Fulton.

Drummond, MJ (1998) Observing Children, in Smidt, S (ed.) *The Early Years: A Reader.* London: Routledge.

Drummond, MJ (2003) *Assessing Children's Learning* (2nd ed.). London: David Fulton.

Edmiston, B (2008) *Forming Ethical Identities in Early Childhood Play.* London: Routledge.

Elfer, P (2005) Observation matters, in Abbott, L and Langston, A (eds.) *Birth-to-Three Matters.* Maidenhead: Open University Press.

Elliott, J (1998) *The Curriculum Experiment: Meeting the challenge of social change.* Buckingham: Open University Press.

Ellis, E (2004) *Exemplars of curriculum theory.* New York: Eye on Education.

Erikson, EH (1963) *Childhood and Society* (2nd ed.). New York: Norton.

Erikson, EH (1982) *The life cycle completed: A review.* New York: Norton.

Eysenck, MW (1995) *Principles of cognitive psychology.* London: Royal Holloway University of London.

Faragher, J and MacNaughton, G (1998) *Working with young children* (2nd ed.) Melbourne: RMIT Publications.

Farrell, A (2005) (ed.) *Ethical Research with Children.* Maidenhead: Open University Press.

Feldman, A (1997) Varieties of wisdom in practice of teachers, in *Teaching and Teacher Education*, 13 (7): 757–773.

Field, F (2010) *The Foundation Years: Preventing Poor Children Becoming Poor Adults*, available at: **www.bristol.ac.uk/ifssoca/outputs/ffreport.pdf** (accessed 25 October 2011).

Fielding, NG and Fielding, JL (1986) *Linking Data: Qualitative Research Methods Series.* Vol. 4. London: SAGE.

Fitzgerald, D and Kay, J (2008) *Working Together in Children's Services.* London: Routledge.

Foucault, M (1961) *Madness and Civilisation: A History of Insanity in the Age of Reason* (trans.) Howard, R. London: Routledge

Foucault, M (1977) *The Archaeology of Knowledge* (trans.) Sheridan, AM. London: Tavistock.

Freire, P (1970) *Pedagogy of the Oppressed.* New York: Seabury Press.

Freire, P (1970) *Cultural Actions for Freedom.* Cambridge, MA: The Harvard Educational Review.

Freire, P (1973) *Education for Critical Consciousness.* New York: Seabury Press.

Freire, P (1978) *Pedagogy in process: The letters to Guinea-Bissau*, trans. C St John Hunter. New York: Seabury Press.

Freire, P (1978a) *Education for Critical Consciousness.* New York: Seabury Press.

Freire, P (1978b) *Pedagogy in Process: The Letters to Guinea-Bissau* (trans. St. John Hunter, C). New York: Seabury Press.

Freire, P (1982) *Pedagogy of the Oppressed*, trans. MB Ramos. Harmondsworth: Penguin.

Freire, P (1994) *Pedagogy of Hope: Reliving Pedagogy of the Oppressed*, trans RP Barr. New York: Continuum.

Freire, P (1998) *Teachers as cultural workers: Letters to those who dare to teach.* Boulder, CO: Westview Press.

Freire, P (2001) *The Pedagogy of the Oppressed* (30th anniversary ed.). London and New York: Continuum.

Freud, S (1923) *An outline of psychoanalysis.* London: Hogarth.

Freud, S (1933) *New introductory lectures in psychoanalysis.* New York: Norton.

Freud, S (1964) An outline of psychoanalysis, in Stracehy, J (ed. and trans.) *The standards edition of the complete psychological works of Sigmund Freud*, vol. 23. London: Hogarth Press (original work published 1940).

Gillham, B (2008) *Observation Techniques: Structured to Unstructured*, London: Continuum.

Giroux, HA (2011) *On Critical Pedagogy.* London: Continuum.

Glassman, WE (2000) *Approaches to psychology* (3rd ed.). Buckingham: Open University Press.

Guba, EG (1985) The context of emergent paradigm research, in Lincoln, YS (ed.) *Organisational theory and inquiry: the paradigm revolution.* Beverly Hills, CA: SAGE.

Guba, EG (1987) What have we learned about naturalistic evaluation?, in *Evaluation Practice*, vol. 8: 23–43.

Gubrium, JF and Holstein, JA (1997) *The new language of qualitative method.* New York: Oxford University Press.

Hall, S (1997) Subjects in History: Making Diasporic Identities, in Wahneema, L (ed.) (1997) *The House that Race Built.* New York: Pantheon.

Hamilton, C, Haywood, S, Gibbins, S, McInnes, K and Williams, J (2003) *Principles and Practice in the Foundation Stage,* Learning Matters.

Hammersley, B (1996) The relationship between qualitative and quantitative research: paradigm loyalty versus methodological eclecticism, in Richardson, JTE (ed.) *Handbook of research methods for psychology and the social science.* Leicester: Routledge.

Harcourt, D, Perry, B and Waller, T (2011) *Researching Young Children's Perspectives: Debating the ethics and dilemmas of education research with children.* London: Routledge.

Harlow, HF and Zimmermann, RR (1958). The development of affective responsiveness in infant monkeys, in *Proceedings of the American Philosophical Society*, 102: 501–509.

Harter, S (1996) The development of self-representation, in Damon, W and Eisenberg, N (eds.) *Handbook of child psychology: Social, emotional and personality development* (5th ed.). New York: Wiley.

Hartley, D (1993) *Understanding the Nursery School: A Sociological Analysis.* London: Cassell.

Hendrick, H (1997) Construction and Reconstruction of British Childhood: An Interpretive Survey, 1800 to present, in James, A and Prout, A (2nd ed.) *Constructing and Reconstructing Childhood: Contemporary issues in the sociological study of childhood*, (1997) 34–63. London: Falmer Press.

Her Majesty's Government (2004) *The Children Act 2004.* London: HMSO.

Her Majesty's Government (2006a) Children's workforce strategy: Building a world class workforce for children, young people and families. The Government Response to the Consultations. London: DfES.

Her Majesty's Government (2006b) The common assessment framework for children and young people: practitioner's guide. London: The Stationery Office.

Hobart, C and Frankel, J (2004) *A Practical Guide to Child Observations and Assessments* (3rd ed.). Cheltenham: Stanley Thornes.

House, ER (1994) Integrating the quantitative and qualitative, in Reichardt, CS and Rallis, SF (eds.) *The qualitative-quantitative debate: New perspectives.* San Francisco: Jossey-Bass.

Howard, K and Sharp, JA (1983) *The Management of a Student Research Project,* Aldershot: Gower.

Howe, KR (1988) Against the quantitative-qualitative incompatibility thesis or dogmas die hard, in *Educational Researcher*, vol. 17: 10–16.

Hughes, JA (1990) *The philosophy of social research* (2nd ed.). Horlow: Longman.

Hurst, V (1991) *Planning for Early Learning.* London: Paul Chapman Publishing.

Illich, I (1970) *Deschooling Society.* New York: Harper and Row.

Isaacs, S (1930) *The intellectual growth on young children.* London: Routledge.

Isaacs, S (1933) *Social Development in Young Children.* London: Routledge.

Isaacs , S (1935) *Psychological Aspects of Child Development.* London: Evans.

Isaacs, S (1948) *Childhood and after.* London: Routledge and Kegan Paul.

James, A and Prout, A (1997) *Constructing and reconstructing childhood* (2nd ed.). London: Falmer.

Keat, R and Urry, J (1975) *Social Theory as Science*. London: Routledge and Kegan Paul.

Kelly, AV (2009) *The curriculum: Theory and Practice* (6th ed.). London: SAGE.

Kerlinger (1970) *Foundations of behavioural research*. New York: Holt, Rinehart & Winston.

Kjorholt, AT (2001) 'The participating child': a vital pillar in this century?, in *Nordissk Pedagogic*, vol 21: 65–81.

Kjorholt, AT (2002) Small is powerful: discourses on 'children and participation' in *Norway, Childhood*, vol 9 (1): 63–82.

Klahr, D (1992) Information processing approaches to cognitive development, in Bronstein, MH and Lamb, ME (eds.) *Developmental psychology: An advanced textbook* (3rd ed.) 3–58.

Kliebard, H (2004) *The struggle for the American curriculum: 1983–1958*. New York: Taylor and Francis.

Kuhn, TS (1970) *The structure of scientific revolutions* (2nd ed.). Chicago: University Press of Chicago.

Lally, M and Hurst, V (1992) Assessment in Nursery Education: a preview of approaches, in Blenkin, GM and Kelly, AV (ed.) *Assessment in Early Childhood Education* (1992), 69–93. London: Paul Chapman.

Layder, D (1993) *New strategies in social research*. Cambridge: Polity.

Laevers, F (1994) The Leuven Involvement Scale for Young Children [manual and video]. Leuven, Belgium: Centre for Experiential Education; 1994. Experiential Education Series, No. 1.

Laevers, F (1997) Assessing quality of childcare provision: 'Involvement' as criterion, in Settings in interaction, in *Researching Early Childhood*, vol 3: 151–165. Goteborg University.

Laevers, F (1998) Understanding the world of objects and of people: Intuition as the core element of deep level learning, in *International Journal of Educational Research*, vol 29 (1): 69–85.

Laevers. F (1999) The project Experiential Education: Well being and involvement – name the difference, in *Early Education*, no. 27. Discussion paper.

Laevers. F (2000) Forward to basics! Deep-level learning and the experimental approach, in *Early Years*, vol 20 (2): 20–29.

Laevers, F (ed.) (2005) *Well-Being and Involvement in Care Settings. A Process-oriented Self-evaluation Instrument Research Centre for Experiential Education*. Leuven, Belgium: Leuven University.

Laevers, F (2005) The curriculum as means to raise the quality of ECE. Implications for policy. *European Early Childhood Education Research Journal* 2005; 13(1): 17–30.

Laevers, F (2009) *Improving quality of care with well-being and involvement as the guide. A large scale study in Flemish setting*. Final report. Leuven, Belgium: Kind & Gezin, CEGO Leuven University.

Laevers, F, Bogaerts, M and Moons, J (1997) *Experiential education at work. A setting with 5-year olds* [manual and video]. Leuven, Belgium: Centre for Experiential Education.

Laevers, F and Moons, J (1997) Enhancing well-being and involvement in children. An introduction in the ten action points [videotape]. Leuven, Belgium: Centre for Experiential Education.

Lincoln, YS (1990) The making of a constructivist, in Cuba, E (ed.) *The paradigm dialog*, 67–87. Newbury Park, CA: SAGE.

Lincoln, YS (1994) The fifth moment, in Denzin, NK and Lincoln, YS (eds.) *Handbook of Qualitative Research*. Thousand Oaks, CA: SAGE.

Local Safeguarding Children Board Regulations (2006) **www.legislation.gov.uk/uksi/2006/90/contents/ made** (Accessed 17 April 2012).

Lorenz, K. (1935) Der Kumpan in der Umwelt des Vogels. Der Artgenosse als auslösendes Moment sozialer Verhaltensweisen, in *Journal für Ornithologie* 83: 137–215, 289–413.

Luff, P (2007) Written observations or walks in the park: Documenting children's experiences, in Moyles, J (ed.) *Early Years Foundations: Meeting the Challenge*. Maidenhead: Open University Press.

Lyotard, JF (1979) *The Postmodern Condition.* Minneapolis, MN: University of Minnesota Press.

MacNaughton, G (ed.) (2003) *Shaping Early Childhood, Learners, Curriculum and Contexts.* Maidenhead: Open University Press.

Malaguzzi, L (1993) For an education based on relationships, in *Young Children,* November, 9–13.

Malaguzzi, L (1995) History, ideas and basic philosophy: An interview with Lella Gandini, in Edwards,C, Gandini, L and Froman, G (eds.) *The Hundred Languages of Children: The Reggio Emilia Approach to Early Childhood Education.* United States: Ablex Publishing Corporation.

Malaguzzi, L (1996) The Hundred Languages of children: A narrative of possible (catalogue of the exhibit). Reggio Emilia, Italy: Reggio Children.

Male, T and Palaiologou, I (2012) Learning-Centred Leadership or Pedagogical Leadership? An alternative approach to leadership in education contexts, in *International Journal of Leadership in Education,* vol 15 (1): 107–118.

Marsh, CJ (2004) *Key concepts understanding curriculum.* London: Routledge.

Marton, F and Booth, S (1997) *Learning and Awareness.* Mahwah, NJ: Lawrence Erlbaum.

Maykut, P and Morehouse, R (1994) *Beginning qualitative research: a philosophic and practical guide.* London: The Falmer Press.

Miles, M and Huberman, M (1994) *Qualitative data analysis: An expanded sourcebook* (2nd ed.) Thousand Oaks, CA: SAGE.

Miller, L and Cable, C (2010) *Professionalisation, Leadership and Management in the Early Years.* London: SAGE.

Miller, L and Havey, D (2012) *Policy Issues in the Early Years.* London: SAGE.

Miller, L, Hughes, J, Roberts, A, Paterson, L and Staggs, L (2003) Curricular guidance and frameworks for the early years: UK perspectives, in Devereux, J and Miller, L (eds.) *Working with children in the early years* (2003), 103–113. London: David Fulton Publishers Ltd.

Mills, J and Mills, R (2000) *Childhood Studies: A reader in perspectives of childhood* (ed.). London: Routledge Falmer.

Ministry of Education (1996) *Te Whaariki. He Whaariki Matauranga mo nga Mokopuna O Aoteroa. Early Childhood Education,* Learning Media. **www.minedu.govt.nz/web/downloadable/dl3567_v1/whariki.pdf** (accessed December 07).

Mohanty, C (1989) On race and voice: Challenges for Liberal Education in the 1990s, in *Culture Critique,* vol 14 (192): 179–208.

Montessori, M (1912) *The Montessori Method* (trans.) Anne Everett George (1882–). New York: Frederick A. Stokes Company.

Montessori, M (1967) *The Absorbent Mind.* New York: Delta.

Montessori, M (1969) 'The Four Planes of Development'. *AMI Communications* (2/3): 4–10.

Moore, K (2001) *Classroom teaching skills* (5th ed). Oxford: Heinemann.

Morgan, DL (1998) Practical strategies for combining qualitative and quantitative methods: Applications for health research, in *Qualitative Health Research,* vol. 8 362–376.

Moyles, J (1989) *Just playing? The role and status of play in early childhood education.* Milton Keynes: Open University.

Moyles, J (2005) *The excellence of play* (2nd ed.). Maidenhead: Open University Press.

Moyles, J (ed.) (2007) *Early Years Foundations: Meeting the Challenge.* Maidenhead: Open University Press.

Moyles, J (ed.) (2010) *Thinking About Play: Developing a Reflective Approach.* Maidenhead: Open University Press.

Moyles, J (2010) *The Excellence of Play* (3rd ed.). Maidenhead: Open University Press.

Moyles, J, Adams, S and Musgrove, A (2002) *The Study of Pedagogical Effectiveness, A Confidential Report to the DfES.* Chelmsford: Anglia Polytechnic University.

Moyles, J, Hargreaves, L, Merry, R, Paterson, F and Esartes-Sarries, V. (2003). *Interactive teaching in the primary school: Digging deeper into meaning.* Maidenhead: Open University Press.

Munro, E (2011) *The Munro Review of Child Protection Report: A Child-centered System*, available at: **www.martmotreview.org** (accessed 18 January 2012).

New Zealand Ministry of Education (1996) *Te Whariki. HE Whariki Matauranga monga-Mokopuna o Aotearoa: Early Childhood Curriculum.* Wellington: Learning Media.

Nurse, A (2007) *The New Early Years Professional.* London: Routledge.

Nurse, A (2008) *The New Early Years Professional.* London: Routledge

Nutbrown, C (2007) *Threads of thinking* (2nd ed.). London: Paul Chapman.

Nutbrown, C (2012) Early Years qualification review interim report. **www.education.gov.uk/nutbrownreview** (accessed March 17 2012)

Nutbrown, C and Carter, C (2010) The tools of assessment: watching and learning, in G Pugh and D Duffy (eds.) *Contemporary Issues in the Early Years* (5th edition). London: SAGE.

Nutbrown, K (2006) *Key concepts in early childhood education and care.* London: SAGE.

OECD (2011) Early Childhood Education and Care. **www.oecd.org/edu/earlychildhood** (Acessed 17 April 2012).

Owen, S and Haynes, G (2010) 'Training and workforce issues in the early years', in *Contemporary Issues in the Early Years* (5th ed.). London: SAGE.

Oxford English Dictionary (OED) (2011). Oxford: Oxford University Press.

Palaiologou, I (2010) Personal Social and Emotional Development, in Palaiologou, I (ed.) (2010) *Early Years Foundation Stage: theory and practice.* London: SAGE.

Palaiologou, I (2011) '*Transdisciplinarity in early years: A Case for doxastic pedagogy?*' Paper presented at British Early Childhood Education and Care Conference. Birmingham, England (February 2011).

Palaiologou, I (ed.) (2012) *Early Years Foundation Stage: Theory and Practice* (2nd ed.). London: SAGE.

Palaiologou, I (2012a) Introduction: Towards an Understanding of Ethical Practice in Early Childhood, in Palaiologou, I (ed.) (2012) *Ethical Practice in Early Childhood.* London: SAGE.

Palaiologou, I (2012b) Ethical Praxis When Choosing Research Tools for Use with Children Under Five, in Palaiologou, I (ed.) (2012) *Ethical Practice in Early Childhood.* London: SAGE.

Papatheodorou, T, Luff, P and Gill, J (2011) *Child Observation for Learning and Research.* Essex: Pearson Education.

Papatheodorou, T and Moyles, J (2009) *Learning together in the early years: Exploring Relational Pedagogy.* London: Routledge.

Penn, H (2005) *Understanding Early Childhood: Issues and Controversies.* Maidenhead: Open University Press.

Pestalozzi, JH (1894) *How Gertrude Teaches her Children* (trans. Lucy E. Holland and Frances C. Turner). Edited with an introduction by Ebenezer Cooke. London: Swan Sonnenschein.

Piaget, JJ (1929) *The child's conception of the world.* New York: Harcourt Brace.

Piaget, JJ (1952) *The origins of intelligence in children.* New York: International Universities.

Piaget, JJ (1954) *The construction of reality in the child.* New York: Basic Books.

Piaget, JJ (1962) *Play dreams, and imitation in childhood.* New York: WW Norton.

Piaget, JJ (1965) *Child's conception of language.* London: Routledge and Kegan Paul.

Piaget, JJ (1968) *On the development of memory and Identity.* Clark University Press: Barre.

Piaget, JJ (1969) *The Child's conception of time.* London: Kegen and Paul.

Pink, S (2007) *Doing Visual Ethnography* (2nd ed.). London: SAGE.

Platt, J (1996) *A history of sociological research methods in America 1920–1960.* Cambridge: Cambridge University Press.

Podmore, VN and Luff, P (2011) *Observation.* Maidenhead: Open University Press.

Pratt, D (1994) *Curriculum Planning: A Handbook for Professionals* (2nd ed.). Forth Worth: Harcourt Brace.

Prior, V and Glaser, D (2006) *Understanding Attachment and Attachment Disorders: Theory, Evidence and Practice.* Child and Adolescent Mental Health, RCPRTU. London and Philadelphia.

Prout, A (2000) Children's participation: control and self-realisation in British late modernity, in *Children and Society*, vol 14: 304–331.

Prout, A (2003) Participation, policy and the changing conditions of childhood, in Hallet, C and Prout, A (2003) (eds.) *Hearing the voices of children: Social policy for a new century.* London: Routledge Falmer.

Pugh, G (2010) The Policy Agenda for Early Childhood Series, in Pugh, G and Duffy, B (eds.) (2010) *Contemporary Issues in the Early Years: Working Collaboratively for Children* (4th ed.). London: SAGE.

Puonti, A (2004) *Learning to work together: collaboration between authorities in economic-crime investigation.* PhD Thesis: University of Helsinki, Department of Education, Centre for Activity Theory and Developmental Work Research. Helsinki: University of Helsinki.

QCA/DfEE *Qualifications and Curriculum Authority/Department for Education and Employment* (2000), Curriculum Guidance for the Foundation Stage. London: QCA.

Reichart CS and Rallis SF (eds.) (1994) *The qualitative-quantitative debate: New perspectives.* San Francisco: Jossey-Bass.

Riddall-Leech, S (2008) *How to observe children* (2nd ed.). Oxford: Heinemann Educational Publishers.

Rinaldi, C (1995) The emergent curriculum and social constructivism: an interview with Lella Gandini, in Edwards, C, Gandini, L and Froman, G (eds.) *The Hundred Languages of Children: The Reggio Emilia Approach to Early Childhood Education.* United States: Ablex Publishing Corporation.

Rinaldi, C (2006) *In dialogue with Reggio Emilia.* London: Routledge.

Rist, RC (1977) On the relations among educational research paradigms: from disdain to détente, in *Anthropology and Education Quarterly*, vol. 8, (2): 42–49.

Roaf, C and Lloyd, C (1995) *Multi-Agency Work with Young People in Difficulty.* Oxford: Oxford Brookes University.

Robinson, M (2008) *Child Development from Birth to Eight: A Journey Through the Early Years.* Maidenhead: Open University Press.

Rodger, R (2003) *Planning an appropriate curriculum for the under fives* (2nd ed.). London: David Fulton Publishers.

Rodger, R (2012) *Planning an Appropriate Curriculum in the Early Years: A guide for early years practitioners and leaders, Students and Parents.* London: Routledge.

Rogoff, B (1998) *Apprenticeship in thinking: cognitive development in social context* (2nd ed.). New York: Oxford University Press.

Rogoff, RC (1990) *Apprenticeship in thinking: Cognitive development in social context.* New York: Oxford University Press.

Rousseau, JJ (1911) *Emile* (trans. Foxley, B). London: Dent.

Salaman, A and Tutchell, S (2005) *Planning educational visits for the early years.* London: SAGE.

Sandra, S (2005) *Observing, assessing and planning for children in the early years.* London: Routledge.

Schaffer, HR and Emerson, PE (1964) 'The Development of Social Attachments in Infancy'. *Monographs of the Society for Research in Child Development,* 29, 94.

Schiro, MS (2008) *Curriculum Theory: Conflicting visions and enduring concerns:* London: SAGE

Scott, D (2008) *Critical essays on major curriculum theorists.* London: Routledge.

Seefeldt, C (1990) Assessing Young Children, in Seefeldt, C (ed.) (1990) *Continuing issues in early childhood education.* Upper Saddle River, NJ: Merrill/Prentice Hall.

Shaffer, D and Kipp, K (2007) *Developmental Psychology: Childhood and Adolescence* (7th ed.). Belmont: Thomson and Wadsworth.

Silber, K (1960) *Pestalozzi: The Man and his Work.* London: Routledge and Kegan.

Silverman, D (1985) *Qualitative methodology and sociology: Describing the social world.* Aldershot: Gower.

Silverman, D (1993) *Interpreting Qualitative data: Methods for analysing qualitative data.* London: SAGE.

Silverman, D (2011*) Interpreting Qualitative Data: Methods for analysing qualitative data* (4th ed.). London: SAGE.

Simpson, M and Tunson, J (1995) *Using observations in small-scale research.* Glasgow: GNP Booth.

Siraj-Blatchford, I and Sylva, K (2002) *The effective pedagogy in the early years project: A confidential report to the DfES.* London: London University Institute of Education.

Smidt, S (2005) *Observing, assessing and planning for children in the early years.* London: Routledge.

Smidt, S (2007) *A Guide to early years practice* (3rd ed.). London: Routledge.

Smith, AB (1998) *Understanding Children's Development,* (4th ed.). Wellington: Bridget Williams Books.

Smith, JK (1983) Quantitative versus qualitative research: An attempt to clarify the issue, in *Educational Researcher,* vol. 12, 6–13

Smith, JK and Heshusius, L (1986) Closing down the conversation: the end of quantitative-qualitative debate among educational enquires, in *Educational Researcher,* vol. 15, 4–12

Stenhouse, L (1975) *An Introduction to Curriculum Research Development.* London: Heinemann Educational.

Strauss, A (1967) *Qualitative analysis for social scientists.* New York: Cambridge University Press.

Sylva, K, Melhuish, E, Sammons, P and Siraj-Blatchford, I (2001) The Effective Provision of Pre-school Education (EPPE) Project. The EPPE Symposium at BERA Annual Conference, University of Leeds, September 2001.

Sylva, K, Melhuish, EC, Sammons, P, Siraj-Blatchford, I and Taggart, M (2004) *Effective Provision of Pre-School Education (EPPE) Project: Technical Paper 12 The Final Report: Effective Pre-School Education.* London: DfES/Institute of Education, University of London.

Taguchi, HL (2010) *Going beyond the theory/practice divide in early childhood education: Introducing intra-active pedagogy.* London: Routledge.

Tashakkori, A and Teddlie, C (1998) *Mixed methods: combining qualitative and quantitative approaches,* Applied Social Research Methods series, vol. 46. London: SAGE Publications.

Taylor Nelson Sofres with Aubrey, C (2002) *The Implementation of the Foundation Stage in Reception Classes, Confidential Report to the DfES.* Richmond: Taylor Nelson Sofres.

Tedlock, B (2000) Ethnography and ethnographic representation. In Denzin, NK and Lincoln, Y (eds.) *Handbook of qualitative research* (2nd ed.). London: SAGE Publications.

Tickell, C (2011) *The Early Years Foundations for Life, Health and Learning*, available at: **http://media.education.gov.uk/assets/Files/pdf/T/The%20Tickell%20Review.pdf** (accessed 11 December 2011).

Tyler, J (2002) *Te Whaariki: The New Zealand Curriculum Framework*. Available at: **www.worldforumfoundation.org/wf/presentations/index.php?p=2002_tyler** (accessed: December 07).

Tyson, P and Taylor, RL (1990) *Psychoanalytical theories of development: An integration*. New Haven, CT: Yale University.

United Nations (1989) *Convention on the Rights of the Child*. Available at: **www.ohchr.org/english/law/pdf/crc.pdf** (accessed 18 September 2007).

United Nations (1989) *The Convention on the Rights of the Child*. Defense International and the United Nations Children's Fund. Geneva.

Vygotsky, L (1962) *Thought and language*. Cambridge, MA: MIT Press.

Vygotsky, L (1986) *Thought and Language* (2nd ed.). London: The MIT Press, Cambridge.

Waksler, FC (1991) Studying the social worlds of children: Sociological Readings. London: Falmer Press.

Walker, J (1990) *Fundamentals of Curriculum*. New York: Harcourt Brace Jovanovich.

Walker, R (1985) *Applied qualitative research*. Aldershot: Gower.

Warmington, P, Daniels, H, Edwards, A, Leadbetter, J, Martin, D, Brown, S and Middleton, D, (2004) Conceptualizing professional learning for multi-agency working and user engagements, paper presented at British Educational Research Association Annual Conference, University of Manchester, 16–18 Sept 2004.

Watkins, C and Mortimore, P, (1999) Pedagogy: What do we know?, in Mortimore, P (ed.) (1999) *Understanding pedagogy and its impact on learning*. London: Paul Chapman.

Watson D, Townsley R, and Abbott D (2002) Exploring multi-agency working in services to disabled children with complex healthcare needs and their families, in *Journal of Clinical Nursing*, 11: 367–375.

Webb, EJ, Cambell, DT, Schwartz, RD and Sechrest, L (1996) *Unobtrusive Measures: Nonreactive measures in the social sciences*, Chicago: Rand McNally.

Wellington, JJ (1996) *Methods and Issues in Educational Research*. Sheffield: University of Sheffield.

White, J (1973) *Towards a Compulsory Curriculum*. London: Routledge and Kegan Paul.

White, J (1982) *The Aims of Education Restated*. London: Routledge and Kegan Paul.

White, J (1990) *Education and the Good Life: Beyond the National Curriculum*. London: Routledge and Kegan Paul.

White, J (1990) *Education and Personal Well Being in a Secular Universe*. London: Kegan Page.

White, J (1994) *Education and Personal Well-Being in a Secular Universe*. London: University of London.

Willan, J (2007) Observing Children: Looking into children's lives, in Willan, J, Parker-Rees, R, and Savage, J (2007) (eds.) *Early Childhood Studies* (2nd ed.) Exeter: Learning Matters.

Winnicot, DW (1986) *Holding and Interpretation: Fragment of an analysis*. New York: Hogarth Press.

Winnicot, DW (1987) *The Child, the Family, and the Outside World*. New York: Addison-Wesley Pub Co.

Winnicot, DW (1995) *Maturational Processes and the Facilitating Environment: Studies in the Theory of Emotional Development*, New York: Stylus Pub Llc.

Winnicot, DW (2005) *Playing and Reality*. London: Routledge

Wittgenstein, L (1969) *The Blue and Brown Book*. Oxford: Blackwell.

Wood, E (2010a) Developing integrated approaches to play and learning, in Broadhead, B, Howard, J and Wood, E (2010) (eds.) *Play and Learning in the Early Years: From research to practice*. London: Sage Publications.

Wood, E (2010b) Reconceptualising the play-pedagogy relationship: from control to complexity, in Edwards, S, Brooker, E (eds.) *Rethinking Play.* Maidenhead: Open University Press.

Wood, E and Attfield, J (2005), *Play, Learning and the Early Childhood Curriculum* (2nd ed.). London: SAGE.

Wood, E (ed.) (2008) *The Routledge Reader in Early Childhood Education.* London: Routledge.

Woods, M and Taylor J (1998) *Early Childhood Studies: An holistic introduction.* London: Arnold.

Wright, T (1990) *The Photography Handbook.* London: Routledge.

Appendix

EYPS standards

If you are studying for the EYPS programme, you should be able to address the following standards in each chapter:

Chapter 1: S1, S3 and S5

Chapter 2: S10, S12, S21, S24, and S27

Chapter 3: S11, S13, S16, S22, S23, S33 and S34

Chapter 4: S2, S5, S10, S21, S22 and S23

Chapter 5: S8, S29, S30, S31 and S33

Chapter 6: S1, S10 and S12

Chapter 7: S24, S38 and S39

Chapter 8: S1, S9, S14 and S24

Index

absorbent minds 16
adulthood, preparation for 14
adults, role of 103, 116, 117
Ainsworth, MDS 24–5
Allen, G 6
analysis of observations 84–8
anecdotal records 59t
Aries, P 21
Armstrong, D 127
assemblage 17
assessment *see also* Common Assessment
    Framework
  models 45
  planning 55
  purpose 145–6
  scales 153–4
  types of 145–6
Assessment and Reporting Arrangements 146
attachment theory 23–5, 112
authentic child 12
autonomy 17

Bachmann, M 154
Bandura, Albert 25
bar charts 60t, 79–80
Barad, KK 133
behaviourism 23
Benjamin, AC 43
Benton, M 12
Bernstein, Basil 17, 19
Bick, E 22, 120
Birth to Three Matters (DfES) 5
Booth, S 10
Bourdieu, Pierre 17
Bowlby, John 24–5, 112, 120
Brandon, M 104
Brewer, J 127
Bronfenbrenner, Urie 26–7, 139
Brown, K 151
Brownlee, J 133
Bruner, J 19, 132
Bryman, A 122, 124
Burgess, RG 122

Carr, M 45–6, 139
Carter, C 42
checklists 60t, 72–6
'Child and Young People's Development' (HMG) 150
child as apprentice 14
child-as being 12
child as child 12
child as imitative learner 19
child as noble savage 21
child-as-project 12
child development

areas of 34–5, 107–10
holistic approach 107
overview 33–4
philosophical ideas 15–19
psychological theories 21–33
skills 149
socio-constructions 11–15
child in need of protection 14
child involvement 53–4, 72, 82, 101–2
child of the welfare state 12
child protection 3, 103
child-study child 12
childhood, theories of 11–15
Children Act 2004 1, 2, 44
children as animals 13
children as apprentice 13
children as innocent 13
children as members of a distinct group 13
children as persons in their own right 13
children as vulnerable 13
children of the nation 12
Children's Centres 150
Children's Workforce Development Council
    (CWDC) 4
Clark, A 53–4
classroom design 29
climate of listening 54
code of practice 99
cognition 27–32
cognitive development 16, 109t
cognitive psychology 27–8, 32, 115, 120
Common Assessment Framework (CAF) 1, 3–4,
    40–1, 103–4, 152–3
common assessment processes 40–1
Common Core of Skills and Knowledge 7,
    149–50, 151
communication 34, 44, 45, 92, 139, 149
community liaison 11, 137, 139, 143
competent learner 107
consent 98–100
creative development 35
creativity 110t
critical pedagogy 17, 18, 132–3
curriculum
  approaches to 134–5
  early years setting 141–2
  ideologies of 134
  observation and 144
  observing for 143–5
  pedagogy and 19, 132–3, 135–40
Curriculum Guidance 38

Dahberg, G 12
Darwin, C 21
data collection methods 127–8

Data Protection Act 1998 103
Datta, L 126
David, T 12
Davies, B 13
Deleuze, Gilles 17
Derrida, J 18–19, 20
developmental child 14
Devereux, J 61
Dewey, John 16
diagrammatic techniques 60t, 76–80
dialogue 16
didactic exposure 19
digital techniques 82, 90–4
diversity 18
documentation 88–96, 103–5, 152–3
  record management 103–5
drawing 101
Drummond, MJ 41

Early Intervention (Allen) 6
Early Learning Goals 7
Early Years Foundation Stage (EYFS)
  aims and objectives 5–6, 14, 145–6, 150–1
  assessment 57, 145–6
  conditions for learning 34–5
  curriculum 141–2
  holistic approach 107, 155
  principles 34, 38, 39, 136
  statutory duties 6–7, 57, 64, 105, 141, 145,
    146, 153
Early Years Foundation Stage Profile 7, 64, 95,
    105, 146, 153–4
Early Years workforce
  Early Years Professional Status 1, 4–5
  as educators and observers 154–6
  multi-agency working 40
  policy context 149–51
  policy context role 151–4
  responsibilities 152, 153–4
  role of 115–16, 117, 136
Early Years Workforce – The Way Forward
    (CWDC) 4
ecology 26–7
ego 22
Elfer, P 44
Elliott, J 135
emotional development 49, 108t, 111–12
emotionalist tradition 123t
empowerment 139
enabling environments 136
Enlightenment 21
epistemic individuals 17
eProfiles 153–4
Erikson, Erik 22
ethics 16, 18
  managing recordings 103–5
  observation process 98–103
  sharing information 105
ethnology 21
ethnomethodological tradition 123t
ethology 24, 25

evangelical child 12
event sampling 59t, 81, 114
Every Child Matters (DfES) 1, 5, 6, 14, 151
  outcomes 2–3, 40, 152
evolution 21
exclusion 18

Fair Society, Healthy Lives (Marmot) 6
family and community 139
Field, F 6
Formative Assessments 145–6
Foucault, Michel 18
The Foundation Years Parenting (Field) 6
freedom 15
Freedom of Information Act 2000 103
freedom to choose 35
Freire, Paulo 18
Freud, Anna 119
Freud, Sigmund 21–2

generalisation 127–8
Gillham, B 42, 96–7
Giroux, Henry 17, 18, 133
Glassman, WE 23
graphic scales 60t, 69–70
guardians, adults as 103
Guba, EG 124
Gubrium, JF 123

Habermas, Jurgen 17
habitus 17
Harlow, HF 24
healthy child 107
Hendrick, H 12
histograms 60t, 78–9
holistic approach 107, 139, 155
Holstein, JA 123
holy child 12
House, ER 126
Howe, KR 127
Huberman, M 127
humanism 16
Hunter, A 127
Hurst, V 87

id 22
ideology 17
Illich, Ivan 16
impolite child 12
innocent child 12, 14
inter-agency work 153
intra-active pedagogy 133
involvement scales 71–2, 91
Isaacs, Susan 15, 40, 119

Key Stage 1 146
Klein, Melanin 119
knowledge and understanding of the world 34
Kohlberg, Lawrence 16

Lally, M 87
lead professionals 3, 4, 7
learner-centred ideology 134

learning and development 136
learning dispositions 140
learning environments 34-6, 41-2, 115-16, 133
learning stories 46, 90, 91, 95-6
Leavers scale 71, 91
Leuven scales 71-2
listening 14, 44
   Mosaic approach 54, 89
   UN 101
literacy 34, 110t
Local Safeguarding Children Board Regulations
      103
Locke, John 21
Lorenz, K 24
Luff, P 44, 52, 94-6, 104
Lyatord, Jean-François 18, 19

Malaguzzi, Loris 137
Male, T 11
March, CJ 134-5
Marmot, M 6
Marton, F 10
mathematics 34
Maykut, P 121, 122
media techniques 82, 92-4
meta-cognitive pedagogy 132
Miles, M 127
Miller, L 2, 36, 138
Mills, J 12-13
Mills, R 12-13
modern child 14-15
Montessori, Maria 16t, 39, 119
Montessori Method 39
moral development 16
Morehouse, R 121, 122
Morgan, DL 124
Mortimore, P 10-11
Mosaic approach 54, 74, 82, 89
Moss, P 53-4
Moyles, J 35, 133
multi-agency working 3, 40, 44, 149, 151, 153
multi-culturalism 143
multicultural curriculum 139-40
The Munro Review of Child Protection Report 6

narratives 59t, 65-8
National Curriculum 141
National Professional Qualification for Integrated
      Children's Centre Leadership (NPQICL) 150
National Standards 5, 150
natural child 12
naturalistic observation 120t
naturalistic tradition 123t
needs, children's 35
New Zealand 45-6, 139-40
non-participant observation
   controlled 23, 120t
   preparation 64-5
   rating scales 68-73
   techniques 59-60t, 65-80
Notes on Infant Observation in Psycho-analytic
      Training (Bick) 22

numeracy 34, 110
numerical scales 60t, 70
Nutbrown, C 42, 149

objectivity 50-2, 54-5, 86-7
observation see also non-participant
      observation; participant observation
   aims and objectives 48-50, 100
   analysis 84-8
   in context 38-40
   for curriculum 143-5
   curriculum and 144
   limitations 96-7
   managing recordings 103-5
   methods of 58-60, 121-8
   nature of 41-2
   objectivity 50-2, 54-5
   origins of 119-21
   in practice 128-9
   purpose 43-5
   reasons for 46-7
   research projects 121-8
   as research tool 120-1t, 129-30
   role of 6-7
Ofsted 4
oppression 18
original sin 21
ownership of learning 35

Palaiologou, I 11
Papatheodorou, T 133
paradigms 125t, 126-7
parental involvement 44, 53, 91, 99-101
participant observation 58t, 60-4, 82
pedagogy
   critical pedagogy 17, 18
   curriculum and 19, 132-3, 135-40
   definitions 10-11
   documentation 92
   psychological theories 21
   philosophical ideas 15-20
   in practice 36
   socio-constructions 11-15
performativity 18, 19
person-centred therapy 16
personal development 109t
personal, social and emotional development 34
Pestalozzi, Johann Heinrich 15
phenomenology 16
philosophical ideas 15-20
photographs 92-4
physical development 34, 108t, 129-30
Piaget, Jean 27, 28-9, 34
pie charts 60t, 79
Pink, S 82
planning 38, 50, 53, 144-5
   questions for 55
Platt, J 127
play 35, 115-16, 119, 141
policy context 149-54
polite child 12
portfolios 64

positive relationships 136
post-modern tradition 123t
poverty 2, 6
power 18, 19
practice theory 17
pre-assessment 152–3
preformationism 21
profiles 7, 64, 95, 105, 146, 153–4
psychoanalysis 21–2, 40–1, 119–20
psychological child 12
psychological methods 15
psychological theories 21, 115
psychosexual theory 21–2
psychosocial development 22
Puritanism 21

qualifications 40
qualitative methods 121, 122–3, 124–8
quantitative methods 123–8

rating scales 60t, 69–72
record management 3–4, 103–5
reflexivity 17
Reggio Emilia 92, 137–8
relational pedagogy 133
relationships 139
reliability 127–8
research projects
    methods of 123–8
    observation and 128–9
    observation as tool 120–1t
    planning 121–2
    theory of 125–6t
responsibility 19
Rinaldi, C 92, 137
Rogers, Carl 16
role play 101, 141
romantic child 12
Rousseau, JJ 21
Rumbold Report 38
running records 59t

safeguarding children 149
sampling 59t, 80–1
sanitised child 12
Schiro, MS 134
scholar-academic ideology 134
schooled child 12
schools, as social institutions 16
Scott, D 135
self-assessment 90–2
self, concept of 111–12
self-observation 74, 121t
semi-structured observation 58t
sharing information 3–4, 44, 90, 91, 105, 149
Silverman, D 122
sinful child 12
skilful communicator 107
Smith, JK 42, 124, 126
social class 17
social cognition 25–6

social control 19
social development 109t, 111–12
social efficiency ideology 134
social environment 22
social inclusion 18
social justice 15
social organisation 17
socially active child 14
socio-constructions of child development 11–13
socio-reconstruction ideology 134
sociograms 60t, 77–8
standards 4–5, 40
story time 101
strong child 107
structured observation see non-participant observation
Summative Assessments 146
superego 22
surveys 124

tabula rasa 21
Taguchi, HL 133
targets 18
Te Whaariki 45–6, 90–1, 139–40, 143
Teaching Agency 4
team involvement 52–3, 99
telematics 19
Ten Years Strategy 141
The Early Years Foundation Stage 1
The Early Years Foundation (Tickell) 6, 40
Tickell, C 6, 40
time sampling 59t, 80
tracking 60t, 76–7
training 6
transitions 146, 149

unique child 136
United Nations Convention on the Rights of the Child (UNCRC) 2, 13, 44, 101
unstructured observation 58t, 60–4

validity 127–8
videos 92–4
violence 25
Vygotsky, Lev 27–8, 30, 137

Walker, R 135
Watkins, C 10–11
well-being scales 71, 91
White, John 17
White, K 151
Willan, J 52
wise practitioner 20
Wittgenstein, Ludwig 16
working together 149
Wright, T 92
written observations see narratives

Youth Matters 3

zone of proximal development 30–1